7/3/15
$35.00
B+T
AS-14
7115

A KURT COBAIN

B MONTAGE OF HECK

A KURT COBAIN
B MONTAGE OF HECK

BRETT MORGEN
WITH RICHARD BIENSTOCK

ORIGINAL ILLUSTRATIONS BY HISKO HULSING
AND STEFAN NADELMAN

INSIGHT ◉ EDITIONS

San Rafael, California

CONTENTS

INTRODUCTION

ALL ARTISTS ARE, IN A SENSE, writing their own autobiographies with their work. Whether one writes about philosophy or paints self-portraits, our life experiences are reflected in and by our creations. I have encountered several amazing artists both in life and through my work. But before I entered Kurt Cobain's archives, I had never experienced or met an artist who expressed himself in so many different media. From the time he was able to pick up a paintbrush, Kurt created. As Krist Novoselic says, "Kurt had to express himself. It just poured out of him."

As a child, Kurt made innocent drawings of his favorite Disney characters. These images convey a sense of idealism and hope. As he got older, he began exploring different media: He began to play and write music, sculpt, make Super 8 films, draw comic strips, and create sound collages and mixed media creations. Kurt's changing views of the world and of himself were always reflected in his creations. Kurt's art is often marked by its raw and kinetic immediacy. He was a bit like an outsider artist; what he lacked in formal training he more than made up for with passion. Kurt's art, whether musical or visual, often had a homemade aesthetic, deeply connected to the underground culture he traveled in throughout the '80s and early '90s. But what truly makes Kurt's work stand out and resonate throughout the world today is his honesty. Few artists of my generation can express how they feel the way Kurt was able to. His work often eschews narrative to arrive at something more primal and real.

OPPOSITE A toy monkey from Kurt Cobain's personal archive

TOP The "Montage of Heck" tape from Kurt's archive

A few years ago, Courtney Love and Frances Bean Cobain approached me about making a documentary on Kurt. While the world knew Kurt Cobain as the lead singer and songwriter of Nirvana, Courtney and Frances were interested in a movie that would explore his other interests as well as create a more multifaceted portrait. They invited me to visit a storage facility that houses all of Kurt's personal artifacts. When I first entered, I encountered dozens of oil paintings, over 4,000 pages of journals, and a box containing over 200 hours of unheard audio cassettes. I later discovered that the box included music, sound collages, spoken word poetry, and a short fictional autobiography that would change the course of my film.

There were boxes of never-before-seen home movies, Super 8 films, and a huge quantity of toys that Kurt had collected throughout his adult life. But Kurt was never content just to own a toy. He had to make it his own. He'd find a way to add something of himself to a board game, doll, or toy monkey. Almost all of his toys looked as if they had emigrated from the island of misfit toys. They looked orphaned and abused—the kind of toys a rich kid would discard as old and ugly. But Kurt was able to see beauty and hope where others saw despair and depravity. Even in his toy collection, Kurt's objects would come to reflect his own unique worldview.

I spent three weeks photographing and documenting all of Kurt's possessions and another two years trying to make sense of everything. Early on I set up two Avid Pro Tools stations to transfer and record the 108 cassette tapes that I found in box 18. As I was pulling out tapes, I discovered cassette 59, which was simply labeled "Montage of Heck." Curious, I put the tape in and pressed play. As I sat surrounded by all of Kurt's earthly possessions and

THESE PAGES A selection of toy monkeys from Kurt's archive

art, I began to experience Kurt's aural masterpiece: a ragtag mash-up of everything from the Beatles to Romanian Polka music. There were snippets of sound from 1970s cartoon shows, scores from horror and sci-fi films, self-realization recordings, music by Simon & Garfunkel and Black Flag, and on and on. In many ways, it felt like the purest expression I had encountered of who Kurt was. It was funny, romantic, harrowing, haunting, playful, contradictory, loud, aggressive, gentle. In short, it was Kurt.

When I set out to make *Kurt Cobain: Montage of Heck*, I wanted to make a film in which Kurt could tell the story of his life through his art, rather than his words. Of all the media Kurt used to express himself during his lifetime, I felt interviews were not his forte. He would come across as either sullen, abrasive, bored, or deceptive. So I set out to create a different kind of movie—one that would bring the viewer into Kurt's world using the art that expressed him best. The "Kurt Cobain experience," if you like.

At some point, I realized that I would need to conduct some interviews with Kurt's family to help contextualize his art. I wanted these interviews to be intimate, soulful, and illuminating. I also did not want them to dominate the film. I was not interested in creating a film in which people sat around talking about Kurt's life. I wanted to create something more experiential. That said, I knew that these interviews would be essential in painting a complete portrait of Kurt.

BELOW Heart-shaped boxes from Kurt's archive

OPPOSITE Selections from Kurt's extensive collection of medical models

While Kurt has been written about and analyzed ad nauseum, the public has rarely, if ever, heard from those who knew him best—his family. *Kurt Cobain*: *Montage of Heck* is the first project that Kurt's mother, father, and sister all agreed to participate in. Their insights into Kurt's formative years will challenge and shatter many of the existing Cobain mythologies, including some which Kurt presented himself.

I often like to say that, if you want to know the history of a subject, read a book. If you want to experience the subject, watch a film. I don't think there is any earth-shattering new information presented in my films *The Kid Stays in the Picture* or *Crossfire Hurricane*, but I believe both films serve a vital and valuable purpose in providing a cinematic experience that takes you into the world of Robert Evans and the Rolling Stones, respectively. Similarly, *Kurt Cobain: Montage of Heck* invites the viewer to experience Kurt in a uniquely cinematic manner. The film isn't interested in "educating" viewers or bombarding them with facts and trivia. It's not a summary of Kurt's biography. Rather, it's a visual expression of Kurt's interior journey through life. It's impressionistic rather than fact-based. If this film is your first introduction to Kurt Cobain, please note that there are many aspects of his story that we could not include. To find out more, I'd suggest that you read a book.

This is that book.

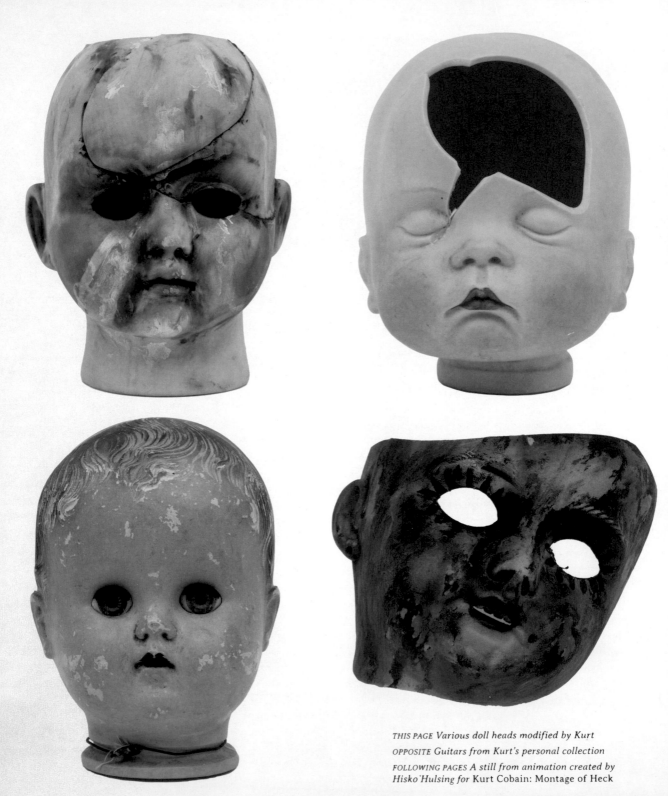

THIS PAGE *Various doll heads modified by Kurt*

OPPOSITE *Guitars from Kurt's personal collection*

FOLLOWING PAGES *A still from animation created by*
Hisko Hulsing for Kurt Cobain: Montage of Heck

14

Kurt Cobain: Montage of Heck, the companion book, brings together the dozens of hours of interview material I amassed for the film and contains many fascinating insights that couldn't find a home in the movie.

Like the film, this book tells Kurt's story. But it tells this story in a very different way and with very different information. I intended for my documentary to be the filmic equivalent of Kurt's aesthetic. It is Kurt from within, whereas this book is a view of Kurt from the outside. Still, it's an incredibly intimate and personal vantage point. It is Kurt through the eyes of the people who knew him best and loved him most. It is Kurt Cobain the son, the brother, the companion, the best friend, the band mate, and, of course, the artist. It is a history, but even here it is a subjective history—one occasionally distorted by emotion, opinion, and the general passage of time. Whether or not I personally condone them, the views expressed in these pages are the opinions of the individuals who were interviewed. As Bob Evans wrote in his book *The Kid Stays in the Picture*: "There are three sides to every story: Your side, my side, and the truth. And no one is lying. Memories shared serve each differently."

I've said this about the film, and I'll say the same about the book: The intention here is not to put Kurt on a pedestal. Nor is it to bring him down. Rather, it is to look him in the eye. To humanize him, for better or for worse.

Kurt has become a myth, in part because nobody really knew him. As a result, we project our collective fantasies onto him. For over twenty years, people have been walking around wearing Kurt Cobain shirts and putting Kurt Cobain posters up in their dorm rooms. But those images are really just a projection, because, outside of his music, Kurt presented only a very limited view of himself to the public. *Kurt Cobain: Montage of Heck*—the film and now also the book—will, I feel, help people to gain a deeper understanding of who Kurt was as a man as well as an artist.

I believe *Kurt Cobain: Montage of Heck* will shatter many of the preexisting mythologies that surround Kurt. And in their wake, as is often the case, a new mythology will be formed. And so it continues.

—Brett Morgen

INTERVIEWEES

The following interviews were conducted in the course of making the documentary *Kurt Cobain: Montage of Heck*. Much of the material was not included in the final film and appears exclusively in this book.

DON COBAIN
Kurt's Father

JENNY COBAIN
Kurt's Stepmother

WENDY O'CONNOR
Kurt's Mother

KIM COBAIN
Kurt's Sister

TRACY MARANDER
Kurt's Girlfriend

COURTNEY LOVE
Kurt's Wife

KRIST NOVOSELIC
Kurt's Friend

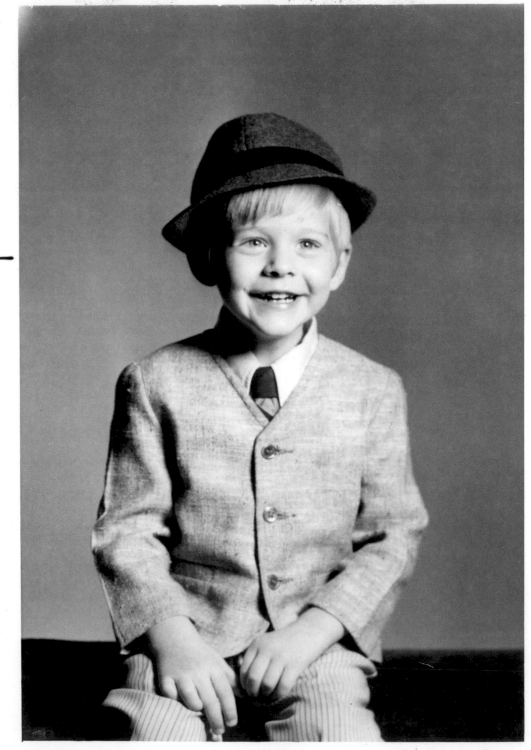

BEEN A SON

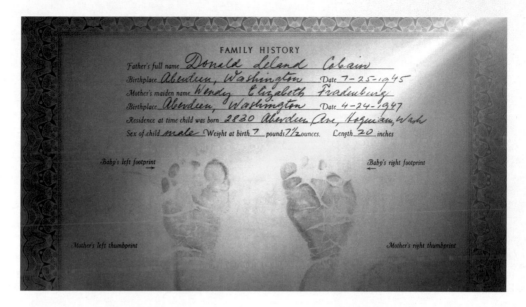

FAMILY HISTORY

Father's full name *Donald Leland Cobain*
Birthplace *Aberdeen, Washington* Date *7-25-1945*
Mother's maiden name *Wendy Elizabeth Fradenburg*
Birthplace *Aberdeen, Washington* Date *4-24-1947*
Residence at time child was born *2830 Aberdeen Ave, Hoquiam, Wash*
Sex of child *male* Weight at birth *7* pounds *7½* ounces. Length *20* inches

Baby's left footprint →
Baby's right footprint ←

Mother's left thumbprint
Mother's right thumbprint

PREVIOUS PAGES
*Animator Hisko
Hulsing's interpretation
of Aberdeen, Kurt
Cobain's hometown*

OPPOSITE *Kurt Cobain at
age three, April 1970*

ABOVE *Kurt's birth
certificate, as seen in*
Kurt Cobain: Montage
of Heck

DON COBAIN: Aberdeen, Washington, was a logging town. I worked for a logging company, too. My second job. It was pretty booming then when I was there, up until the '60s. Then I went to work in a gas station, and then I went to another logging company. That's when the logging was very big, but then the bottom fell out of it. Everybody lost their jobs, and I think everybody's been losing their jobs ever since then.

WENDY O'CONNOR: I lived in Cosmopolis [Washington, a seven-minute drive from Aberdeen]. My uncle owned two mills. There were tugboat companies and mills and just anything to do with wood, plywood, shingles. It was the best of times. Even though we didn't have much, we were always able to get what we needed. So it was really good.

DON: I think I was two years older than Wendy. We met in high school, started dating, and everything went from there. She graduated, and then I graduated from junior college. I was gonna go on to four-year college, but I didn't have the money. And my parents didn't help me so I did the next thing: got married. That's what you did then. If you didn't do anything else, you got a job, got married. So we went to Idaho because you can get married there. You know, she was just 18.

WENDY: I didn't know what falling in love was, so I had never experienced it. So I just thought because I liked him, I loved him. And so he got me an engagement ring, and we got engaged. You know, it was fun! I mean it was, like, "Okay, all those problems are behind me. Now I'm going to have babies!" And I just couldn't wait to get pregnant. I used to think, "Why did I marry Don Cobain?" You know? And I was like, no, everything really did happen for a reason. Kurt had to be born.

DON: It was a new experience for us, but we did everything a husband and wife do with a kid. What I most remember about Kurt when he was little is probably when he dressed up in the suit and the hat and everything. I guess he was probably about two years old. At Christmastime, he would put on a little suit, play drums. That's how I remember Kurt the most. I think of the little guy dressed up in his suit, playing drums.

WENDY: He was banging on pots and pans at, like, six months. Most children do that, though. So we got him a little drum and drumsticks at probably ten months. And he was always, like, if music was on, he would always go to the beat. We would meet at least once a month at one of our houses, and it ended up being my brother Chuck's most of the time because he built stereos and he was a mathematician. He could just do anything. And so he had all this equipment in his basement for recording. He had drum

"At Christmastime, he would put on a little suit, play drums." —DON

When Kurt was born, and then Kim, his sister . . . I loved raising children in [Aberdeen], because it was small enough to where you could keep track of them but big enough to where you had two movie theaters and a lot of stores, and I just loved it.

ABOVE A young Don Cobain in 1966

LEFT Don Cobain is interviewed for Kurt Cobain: Montage of Heck

OPPOSITE Selections from Cobain family footage of the young Kurt

OPPOSITE *Various scenes of the young Kurt taken from Cobain family footage*

BELOW LEFT AND RIGHT *The young Wendy O'Connor*

BOTTOM *Wendy being interviewed for the documentary in 2014*

sets and recording gear and an echo chamber, and it was really fun. And Kurt participated in all of that. He just showed, as the rest of us did, love for music right away—within the first year. You know, he wanted a guitar, he wanted a drum set, he always wanted musical instruments. But he wanted trucks and planes and bikes and all that kind of stuff, too. But he just really loved music. It was just the way it was in our family.

DON: He was a little towhead, cute little kid, and he was very entertaining. He would perform. He did dances and stuff and dressed up. He put on little shows all the time. It was very encouraged by Wendy's side of the family.

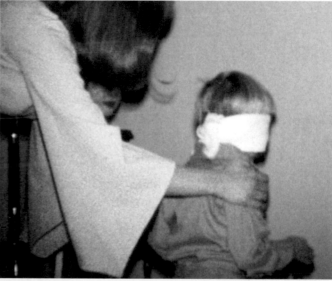

WENDY: I was doing tole painting when he was probably eight months, seven months. And he was always wanting to get up and sit on my lap, so I'd always give him a piece of paper, and he'd just sit next to me. He'd have his pencil, and he'd be kind of mimicking me and doing that. And I noticed that he was drawing really good circles, so then I took his hand with his pencil in it and showed him how to do eyes. I'm not real sure how young he was. He was young, though. Ten months, something like that. As we continued doing all that, he got really good. And my brother Chuck, one day he came to the house and saw that Kurt had done Pluto and all the Disney characters, and he said, "Kurt, could you draw me, like, Mickey Mouse?" And Chuck said, "Wendy, look at this." He goes, "He's not drawing like most people do." He drew, like, his nose first, then his ears. Like, most kids would draw a head, and they'd add ears and a nose and a mouth and whatever. He had specific parts of the face or whatever it was, and he would draw those first and then fill everything else in. And it was really interesting to watch him do that.

KIM COBAIN: He was so praised as a kid as an artist. With drawing and painting, he liked it all, and he could do it and it just came so easy to him. And he didn't understand. I don't think he understood, like, "What's the big fuss?" I mean, it was just there. And I think that because we all saw what a great artist he was, everybody got him art supplies, you know, for every birthday, every Christmas.

WENDY: Anytime his little sister cried, it would bother Kurt. Babies cry sometimes for no reason, but that would upset him and he would run right into her room and make sure everything was okay. He just was a good kid. He was sweet, gentle. I'm not painting a picture of him being a little, you know, perfect child, because, I mean he could get into it and fight with Kim and other kids, too. He wasn't a pushover. But he was just sensitive to other children's needs.

DON: Kurt, you know, I don't think people realized how sensitive he was.

WENDY: I don't think Kurt was too sensitive. The word "sensitive" to me is: "Everybody is hurting me, everybody is hurting me." He wasn't like that. He played fair, and he wanted everyone else to play fair. And he would get mad. I mean, he wouldn't cry about it, and he wouldn't whine about it. He would be mad.

KIM: He was extremely protective. From the time he was two years old and could notice that guys were looking at mom, he was flipping them off. Mom would be driving, and he'd see some guy looking in the car window at her, and he'd flip him off.

"When I was young, I was kind of bullied by some guys one time, and [Kurt] went and punched one of them in the face."—KIM

WENDY: And that started at a very, very young age. He started doing that, like, when men would look at me. I don't think he was protecting his dad's woman. I think he was protecting me from other men. He didn't want men looking at me. And two guys that I know, I knew their wives, they said, "Hey, Wendy, did you know when you guys were coming down over the bridge the other day, do you know that Kurt was sitting in the back seat, and when I looked over and waved at you, he gave me the finger?" And I went, "No . . ." And he goes, "Yeah." And then another guy told me the same thing, so it was, like, "Hey, don't look at my mom." He wasn't a momma's boy, though. He'd get really, really mad at me about things. But I know that he loved women. He just thought they were the greatest, even my mother. He really respected her, and he was always very polite and kind. So, yeah. He was a protector. Of women and women's rights.

KIM: When I was young, I was kind of bullied by some guys one time, and [Kurt] went and punched one of them in the face. I didn't know for months that he had done that until the guy came up to me and was, like, "Yeah, your brother punched me in the face for you." And I'm, like, "What?"

WENDY: Boy, if anybody messed with Kim, he was right at their front door ready to punch them out.

KIM: And he was always flipping the bird. I don't know where he got it. My very first memory is with my brother, and we were outside, and I was probably three, and I'm in my little pink fluffy dress, and he's got me flipping off the cops as they go by. And as my mother says, the cop came around the block and knocked on the door after Kurt and I ran in the house. And he said, "You know your son is out in the yard having your poor little daughter flipping the

TOP *The young Kurt was a big fan of superheroes*

OPPOSITE *Sports car art by the young Kurt*

bird to the cops." And then as we grew up, he'd yell out at the cops, like, "Corn on the cops! Corn on the cops!" And he thought that was hilarious.

DON: He was always sorta hyper. He would go miles an hour almost all the time. I guess he was on Ritalin. But, see, I don't remember that stuff.

WENDY: The ADHD? [That started at] about three. Two and a half. Just about three. He would just be full of too much energy, just rocking, banging against the wall, upside-down watching *Sesame Street*, you know, and repeating everything back exactly as it was coming out of the TV. Like his alphabet or whatever it was, counting numbers. Just Speedy Gonzales, you know? And so I took him to the doctor because I think he was about four, four-and-a-half, and he was gonna start kindergarten, and [the doctor] watched him through a two-way mirror. He said that he'd let me stay in the waiting room for about forty-five minutes just to make sure Kurt got to that state, and he did. And then he checked him for Rapid Eye Movement, and he sent me home with three pills. [He] told me to give [them] to him when I got home, which probably would have been late afternoon, and he was up all night. It was the speediest thing. It was sad, but it was hilariously funny at the same time. He kept Don and I up all night long, running into our bedroom with drawings and reading this book to me, just ninety miles an hour, *jabber jabber jabber*. So I called the doctor at, like, five o'clock in the morning and said, "Oh my God, I'm so scared. His heart's pounding. He's just out of his mind." He says, "Don't give him any more." The next day I went in, and he gave me a prescription for a sedative. So [Kurt] started school and he wasn't running around anymore, but he was very lethargic and he wasn't interested. He wasn't sad or depressed, it was just kind of . . . I liked the old Kurt better. So then I took him back in [to the doctor] and said, "This isn't right. The teacher said he's just lethargic and has his head down on the desk all the time." So he said, "Well, the only other thing I can think of is to cut out his sugar, and no red food coloring." And to this day, that's still the same. I mean, sugar is as addictive as heroin. And food coloring is really bad for the nervous system, the red dye. So I took him off all that and then he was just great. But he felt very deprived because all the other kids got candy and cake and all kinds of other stuff in their lunches, and he never did.

KIM: Kurt, yeah, definitely had a speed-racer mind. Kurt's brain was just constantly going. He was always thinking about something. I mean, there was always something going on.

WENDY: Kurt was hyper. Full of energy. Always busy. You know, jumping off of things, knocking things over. Anything that had to do with being a normal child. And Don, he didn't know how to handle that. He was one of those kind of people that just thought that children should be seen and not heard and shouldn't cause any trouble. I mean, he belittled and ridiculed Kurt. And Kurt would be ashamed. I mean, it really hurt him to be embarrassed.

DON: He just acted out. That's why he was so angry all the time. He didn't have any control. He couldn't express himself.

WENDY: He would kind of, like, grow smaller in size. I don't want to talk against his dad, but his dad did ridicule him in public and it would show on his face. It would hurt him. Don was raised by his dad, [who] was mouthy and loud and cruel to his wife verbally and physically and to Don's two younger brothers. So that's what he watched all his life. Don was just not good to him. I'll give you just one thing that I remember clearly. [Kurt] loved Pizza Pete pizza, and once a month we'd go as a family. And [Kurt] would get all excited and Don was always making everything worse with Kurt in public. He would knuckle rap him on the head all the time, like, "Knock it off Kurt," or pull on his ear, you know? So we were at Pizza Pete and when the waiter came and put Kurt's drink next to him, he put it too close to the edge of the table. Kurt was eating his pizza and he threw his arm back and the drink went all over the place. And Don just flipped out. He was just yelling at him. He made

it so bad, and I was so embarrassed. And this was just typical.

KIM: I barely remember my dad being in the house. I know he did a lot of sports and all that, so he wasn't around in the house a lot. But really, my only images of my dad being there are him in his tighty-whities wandering around the house. And when we watched, [for] the first time, *The Wizard of Oz*, and I was so scared of the flying monkeys and scared of the witch, I was hiding behind my dad. But I was like, four, so I was five when my dad finally moved out.

WENDY: I wanted to get divorced so I could find somebody more suited towards me that wanted to be with me and appreciate me. [Don] never told me I was pretty. He never told me I looked nice, and he never told me he loved me. Ever. Until I broke up with him. We broke up in the winter of '79, and he went and lived with his mom and dad, and then we [got] back together, which was just stupid. I mean, he wore me down, made me feel bad, guilty, and then right back to getting divorced again.

DON: We were young, you know? I guess I was maybe self-centered or something like that. And sports, maybe she didn't like going to all those tournaments every weekend. I played on the city basketball team. So maybe I left her with the kids too long. She wanted a divorce, and I said, "Okay." I didn't want to upset the apple cart. That's the way I do things. I just put everything inside me or behind me or just let it go. I don't think about it.

WENDY: The kids were gonna stay with me at the house. And then Kurt was nine at the time, and he became quite unruly. It just embarrassed him to death that we had gotten divorced. He took light bulbs out

of all the lights and locked the babysitter and Kim outside. He was going into being eleven, and he and Don were getting along really well at that time because he was spending time with his kids for the first time, really. I mean, on the weekends he would come and get them. And he'd spend time with them, and they'd never had that before. So I said, "I called your dad." He hadn't gotten a place, but he was in an apartment. And I said [to Don], "Do you want me to bring him tonight?" And he goes, "Yeah, bring him tonight." I don't think Kurt really minded that. Maybe that's what he wanted me to do. I might have threatened him with it or something. Maybe that's what he wanted.

DON: She couldn't handle him. See, that's the funny thing—I don't like to say bad things and stuff, but she talked bad about me to the kids all the time. And then when Jenny and I got married, when we started having problems with him, we even went to a counselor and they said maybe he didn't feel like he was loved or something like that. So I went and got him legally, and Wendy signed the papers in about two seconds. We thought that maybe that would show him. Because it was suggested to us that that would show a kid he's a part of the family and everything like that.

JENNY COBAIN: He wanted to be in a family, period. And I felt that just from the beginning. The game nights that we had, that was really important to him. You know, if we didn't want to do it on a Wednesday night, you know, he'd say, "Nope! We have to . . ." I could feel that he just really liked that time, but he always wanted to win. And if he didn't win, he was mad. He wanted to be the most loved and it just wasn't the ideal world that he thought a family should be. So, he just decided he wasn't going to do anything anybody said. He'd just lay on the couch and watch TV. Go down in his room and play the guitar.

WENDY: I don't want to put anything on Jenny because she's a sweet girl. But the dynamics between Kurt and Don changed because he found a woman, and then I guess Kurt didn't like her having kids because there was competition.

KIM: My dad remarried and brought in a whole new family and kinda, you know,

TOP Kurt at the age of sixteen with his sister's rabbits Thumper and Rusty

33

didn't want the old family to interfere with the new family. So I think Kurt was kinda pushed to the side, and he got all the blame—'cause he was the oldest—for anything that went wrong. With, like, the stepbrother and stepsister and all that.

DON: He resented it, and he did his own thing. We tried the best we could with him, but, you know, he was a talented person, and I think he was sort of like how geniuses are. He was way, way far ahead of everybody else, and he did his own thing. People who've got a lot of talent like that usually have a little problem. One time I said to him I was never gonna get married again, and I think he took that for a word. I don't know if that did it or what. But I'm easygoing and stuff, and when I had him, it was great. I guess I could have been a better father, but we had a lot of problems with him and I think, you know, he just rebelled.

KIM: Kurt, for some reason, he felt shame about a lot of things. He saw the divorce as a shameful thing for some reason. If he got put down or ridiculed, he really hated it. He just, I mean, nobody likes it, you know, nobody likes to be shamed or made fun of or put down, and he just was extremely hurt by that kind of thing. It made him feel bad about himself.

JENNY: He wanted a mom and a dad, and after he decided maybe that Don was not going to go back with Wendy, I was probably a "step" in [the] right direction at the beginning. And those times were really good. He and I loved music, and for some reason, he actually liked the Pointer Sisters. When "Fire" would come on, we would just go nuts, and he would be beating on stuff and I would be singing with [a] knife. I certainly wasn't a Pointer sister, but he loved anything that had to do with music.

"Kurt, for some reason, he felt shame about a lot of things."—KIM

And when he put on the little plays and skits with Jay [Kurt's stepbrother], I mean, they really set it up, and we were the audience, and we would watch the whole thing. Those were so fun. And Jay was very creative as well, but Kurt was amazing. They would make claymation people. It was in our laundry room, and they had a movie camera with film in it. They would make the film, and then they would show it to us, and they would work on it for days. They had so much fun doing that. And times that we went camping, he really did love that. I mean, it wasn't anything he had ever done before.

DON: When we got married, I couldn't discipline [Jenny's] kids, really, or I was afraid to, 'cause they're not my kids. And her the same way with [Kurt]. But then it got to where she almost had to or else I had to do it to him more, you know, when he started acting out. And he probably resented that and resented the other kids and Jenny, too. Like I was picking on him. But I'd have to be the one to do it because it wasn't her kid.

JENNY: He always wanted the biggest piece of cake and then the biggest taco. He would pile it on. It was more like he didn't think about anybody else in the family. I mean, he was a huge eater for a little guy. That was irritating, because I made dinner for the whole family and one person would eat it all. Trying to talk to him about that was rough.

DON: He was lazy. The kids had chores to do and stuff like that, and he wouldn't do them at times. That was probably the only conflict. He picked on the other kids every once in a while and stuff like that, but I didn't see this stuff most of the time because Jenny was with him and she probably didn't tell me about it. Because, you know, [he was her] stepson.

KIM: My dad, he was a thumper, and he would thump Kurt in the head when he was reprimanding him for anything, if he didn't do the dishes or take out the garbage or whatever.

JENNY: Kurt was sensitive, and [Kurt's half-brother] Chad is pretty sensitive, too. And so they really said, "I don't like him thumping me on the head like that."

DON: I did it to Chad once.

JENNY: That was the last time. I said, "Don't do that!" But he did do that to Kurt. I think it was sort of, like, affectionate in a way. But my kids didn't like it, and Chad didn't like it. And he stopped as soon as he found out he was creating problems for the kids. It wasn't abusive. I can't call it abusive, because it was just

like a little *thump* thing. But, boy, if he got near me and did that I would be so mad at him, because I just thought [it] was the wrong thing to do. And he was just messing around. It wasn't anything serious.

KIM: I mean, [Kurt] got grounded for an entire year because he forgot to feed the dog.

JENNY: I don't think that has ever happened.

DON: Usually they get grounded for a week. I used to get grounded all the time. I was young. All the kids got grounded a week at the most maybe. And you know how that goes, they usually last a week. 'Cause how can you keep a kid in your yard for a week?

JENNY: And it really isn't a realistic thing. We just wouldn't do that, I mean. And how could you, you know?

BELOW Kurt's interest in music began to intensify in his teenage years

SMELLS LIKE TEEN SPIRIT

JENNY: It wasn't till the teenage years with all the kids that it was just different. [Kurt] just changed a lot. He always talked about how people beat him up and stuff. And they picked on him. I didn't see that at all, and his friends didn't see that at all. So that was one of those myths—because he was small, everyone picked on him—but in actuality, he was a bully. So, you start to see these little patterns, do you know what I mean? It's just really eye-opening.

KIM: Oh my god, no. Kurt was never a bully. I can't even imagine him bullying a kid. Not unless it was out of, you know, group mentality that he just kind of was going along with it. The only bullying I got with him was when we were very young and, yes, I was picked on as big brother picking on little sister. And of course, it upset me, and he loved the reaction, you know? But he definitely was not a bully.

JENNY: My son [Jay], after we moved in together, Kurt would beat him up and then kick him in his groin, and Jay wouldn't say anything about it. Then we found out, and I was livid. It was such a horrible thing to see your son all bruised down there. And I thought, What's wrong

with him? Which, you know, the light bulb goes on that there's something wrong here. But we also had a new baby, and [Kurt] really, really enjoyed Chad. I did tell him that I was so proud of how he was with Chad. And Chad really remembers him, and he was pretty darn young.

KIM: He loved our little brother Chad. Oh my god, he adored him. He was so happy when he was born and just adored him. But, you know, with the stepkids it was so different because they were kind of Jenny's little angels.

"So that was one of those myths— because he was small, everyone picked on him—but in actuality, he was a bully."—JENNY

WENDY: You know, Don was an avid sports person. He expected him to do certain things to be a man. To be a guy, to be a boy. I don't think Kurt would've chosen wrestling. I couldn't even believe my ears when [Kurt] said he was wrestling. And then he didn't last long on the baseball field because Don was abusing Kurt verbally, and I saw the look on Kurt's face after a game, and I said, "Do you want to do this?" And he said, "No."

OPPOSITE Kurt at the age of fourteen

JENNY: He was very hypersensitive to criticism. I think he felt like he was being picked on. He was really sensitive, and I think he held everything in him most of the time. He didn't get really angry, ever. I don't remember him ever blowing up. He just sucked it in and then thought about it and maybe could talk about it later. But I felt really badly for him. He was so sensitive.

DON: He was a good baseball player, but he wanted to do [it] his way a lot. One time when he was, I guess, twelve years old, we put him in right field, and supposedly right field's where you put your worst player. And he didn't want to go out there. He threw his glove down and got dejected. So the other coach went and took him out of the game, and they got in a little conflict, and he just took off and went home.

JENNY: I think Kurt from the age of three till the age of twelve was on Ritalin, and we decided to cut it back and then cut it altogether, and he seemed fine. I never

"But I really felt that he had a chemical imbalance of some sort."—JENNY

thought that he was that hyper. I thought he was more lazy than hyper, but maybe the laziness might have been caused by the Ritalin. Who knows? But I really felt that he had a chemical imbalance of some sort. I personally blamed the Ritalin, because he was kind of dependent on it. I was really against that, and I made him stop taking it. I feel a little guilty about that. I called his mom and said, "I just don't think this is right anymore. Seems like he needs to be on his own with his own demons like most people are."

KIM: My dad couldn't handle him. So Kurt went to stay for, like, one week with my uncle Jim, and then he went with my uncle [Chuck], because my mom was in a relationship with, at the time, a boyfriend that was abusive and my mom didn't want [Kurt] around that because he was either gonna end up protecting my mom to where he ends up in jail or you know . . . She didn't want him subjected to that.

TOP A teenage Kurt in 1980 during a visit with his Aunt Mari

OPPOSITE The teenage Kurt's drawings rendered as animation for Kurt Cobain: Montage of Heck

FOLLOWING PAGES An image from Hisko Hulsing's animation shows a teenage Kurt reacting to the presence of one of his mother's boyfriends

JENNY: We were all miserable, every one of us—the kids, Don and I, Kurt—everyone was miserable. It was kind of a very cold environment, and it didn't used to be. We were very affectionate parents. And [Kurt] was very affectionate, too. Which was nice, but he started picking on the kids more, and we were afraid for Chad, even though I swear to this day he absolutely loved that little boy. But [he was] just doing really mean things to the kids, and then doing things at school, and we talked to him about it and he would lie. I think it was kind of my fault in a way, because I couldn't deal with it anymore. And it ended up that I told Don that he's gonna have to go back to his mom's, because I can't do it. So it was more me at that point than it was Don. So we talked to Wendy, and she said, "Well, I'll give it another try."

DON: We tried to handle it as best as we could. But it sort of didn't work out. But there were good times, you know? Everybody has good times and bad times.

"It's hard for me to listen to people put Don down because I know how hard he tried. And it just seems so unfair." —JENNY

And we tried the best we could. That's what we say. Both of us feel—and Jenny has talked about it and said it, too—that maybe we didn't try hard enough.

JENNY: It's hard for me to listen to people put Don down because I know how hard he tried. And it just seems so unfair.

WENDY: Don came to my office; we had a talk. We made a deal to where I would take him Thursday, Friday, Saturday, Sunday, to break it up more. The reason being: I was with a guy for six years. He was brutal. He beat me. It was really bad. And we were in the process of breaking up. He'd gone to another house, I'd kicked him out, and it was quite frightening. I never knew if he was going to show up, and Kurt hated

TOP *Evocative artwork by the teenage Kurt hints at his inner turmoil*

OPPOSITE *A still from a sequence created for the documentary by animator Hisko Hulsing*

FOLLOWING PAGES *A still from Hisko Hulsing's animation showing the young Kurt*

him. When Don finally said, "Jenny can't take it anymore. She's gonna divorce me if you don't take Kurt back," I thought, "Well, okay." So I called Don's brother, Jim—he and I were really good friends in high school, and he's a good guy—I called Jim and asked him if he could take him just until probably two or three months for this guy to leave me alone. [It] worked out good until Jim got into trouble with his wife. So I called my brother Chuck who lived four blocks away from me and asked him if he could take Kurt in. So that was the best thing that could have ever happened for Kurt at that time in his life because this is the brother with the band, the drum set . . . absolutely fantastic parents and he needed to be in a stable family unit where everybody loved him, and it was just the best thing. I said, "Now you let me know when you think he's had enough rehabilitation," because I think that's what he needed. And so I got the call from my brother, and he said, "Wendy, your son needs you."

JENNY: He just was in so much pain that he, you know, took it out on his mom and took it out on his dad and took it out on his siblings. But it's almost like

he didn't feel worthy because he was rejected, basically. And I don't know how anybody deals with having your whole family reject you.

KIM: Chuck had a guitar, and I think he got [Kurt] his first guitar down at Rosevear's [music store].

WENDY: I didn't even know that Chuck had taken him down and got him a guitar. I mean, I wasn't a part of that and then, when [Kurt] showed up, he had, you know, his guitar, and of course we all thought that, if he was going to go musically, [he would take up the] drums, because he was a really good drummer. And it was just great that day that he came down. Summer had just started and, you know, my little protector was home. He's always been my little protector.

KIM: When Kurt was about fifteen, he moved back in. It was me and my mom, and her future husband was there. I don't think [Kurt and he] really had much of a relationship at all. I think they kind of just avoided each other mostly. I mean, my mom's boyfriend knew music, but it

TOP A portrait of Don Cobain drawn by the teenage Kurt

OPPOSITE A delinquent Kurt in a still from a Hisko Hulsing animated sequence

wasn't like he was into music or playing music or understood what Kurt was doing, and I think he just saw him as another lazy teenager that, you know, wasn't doing what he did as a teenager. [As a teenager, mom's boyfriend] was out partying and sleeping around and he was already an alcoholic, and so they had very different lives. And Kurt wasn't real fond of, like, the really kind of super male, testosterone-filled [attitude]. Kurt was much more loving of women instead of wanting to control them or dominate them or just get laid or anything like that. He just wasn't that kind of person.

DON: If he started smoking pot and everything like that, I probably didn't realize it, or Jenny didn't tell me about it. I put it behind my mind. I didn't see him. I know he got in trouble, wasn't where he was supposed to be, wasn't doing what he was supposed to be doing, but I didn't know if he was getting into anything drug related. I really don't remember it.

KIM: You know, it was still him wanting to rebel and getting stoned and going out with his friends and not wanting to do chores. He was always wanting to just do his own thing. He wanted normalcy. He wanted the mom, the dad, and the kids, and everything happy. But then, he didn't, because he kind of fought against it. So he fought against what he really wanted.

WENDY: I lived through the hippie days. I mean, I wasn't stupid. I would check his room. One day I went up to take his clothes up after laundry, and something creaked under the rug and I was, like, "Hmm, that's weird." And so I pull back the rug. It was floorboards, you know, the little thin ones, and he'd cut a little piece out and put his pipe and his pot in there and then put the wood back. So, instead of saying anything to him, I just took it and threw it away. I didn't hear one single word. He acted very strange around me for about a week.

Transcript from Kurt Cobain's private recordings

In a community that stresses macho male sexual stories as the highlight of all conversation, I was [an] underdeveloped, immature little dude that never got laid and was constantly razzed. Oh, poor little kid. It bothered me — probably more so because I was horny and frequently had to make up stories, like, "Uh, when I went on vacation, I met this chick, and we fucked, and she loved it," etc., etc. This typical pubescent problem was a factor in the height of my problems with my father and stepmom. You know, the typical wicked stepmom story. And so I moved to both grandparents' [house] and four sets of aunts and uncles and so forth and so on within the year. And in eighth grade my mom had no choice [but] to take me in because my dad packed my stuff and drove me to her house in the morning and left me there. She was pissed. I accumulated quite a healthy complex, not to mention a complexion. Then one day I discovered the most ultimate form of expression ever: marijuana. Oh boy, pot. I could escape all day long and not have routine nervous breakdowns. Trevor was a guy I hated but resorted to becoming friends with because he was the only person I could get pot from. He was the kingpin. Trevor, Ace, John, Darren — all white trash, low life, scum-of-the-earth, according to the jocks — had been going to this girl's house after school, and they invited me. We got to the door, and a very fat girl let us in. It wasn't obvious to me for over an hour that this girl seemed kind of quiet until one of the guys pointed out that she was in a special ed class. I'm sure a lot of kids would call her a "retard" and some just "slow," and at the time, and still to this day, I would call her quiet and illiterate but not "retarded." The object of the guys who had been going there for the past month was to steal booze from the downstairs basement den of her house. While others distracted her, one would go down and take a fifth and then exit out the downstairs. So we did this routine every other day and got away with it for, oh, about a month. And during that month happened to be the epitome of my mental abuse from my mother. It turned out that pot didn't help me escape my troubles too well anymore, and I was actually enjoying doing rebellious things like stealing booze and busting store windows, and nothing ever mattered. I decided within the next month, I will not sit on my roof and think about jumping, but I'll actually kill myself. And I wasn't going out of this world without actually knowing what it was like to get laid. So one day after school I went to [the] girl's house alone and invited myself in, and she offered me some Twinkies, and I sat on her lap, and I said, "Let's fuck." And I touched her tits, and she went into her bedroom and got undressed in front of me,

50

and I watched and realized that it was actually happening. So I tried
to fuck her but didn't know how and asked her if she had ever done
this before. And she said, "A lot of times," mainly with her cousin.
I got grossed out very heavily with how her vagina smelled, and her
sweat reeked, so I left. My conscience grew to where I couldn't go to
school for a week, and when I went back, I got in-house suspension
for skipping. And that day the girl's father came in screaming and
accusing someone of taking advantage of his daughter. And so, during
lunch, a rumor started, and by the next day everyone was waiting for
me to yell and cuss and spit at me, calling me the "retard fucker."

I couldn't handle the ridicule. So I got high and drunk and walked
down to the train tracks and laid down and put two big pieces of
cement on my chest and legs and waited for the eleven o'clock train.
The train came closer and closer and closer, and it went on the next
track besides me instead of over me. The tension from school had an
effect on me and so I couldn't attend the school anymore. And the
train scared me enough to try and rehabilitate myself and my lifting
weights and, and mathematics seemed to be improving, so I became
less manically depressed but still never had any friends because I,
I hated everyone, for they were so phony.

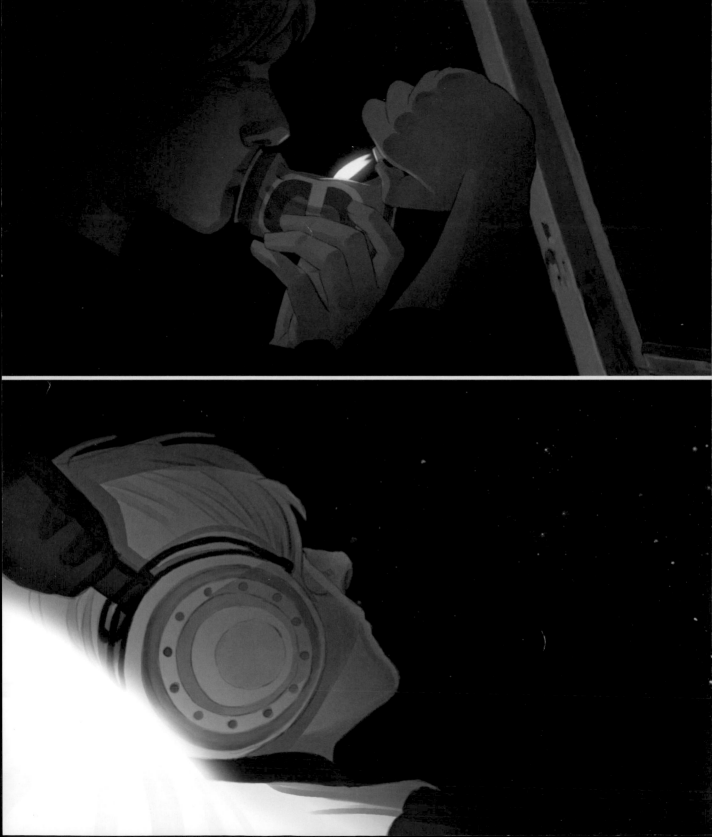

KIM: He was just even more lazy. Wouldn't clean his room. He was just kind of like a curmudgeon. I think it was kind of typical teenage shit, but it was also, like, "I just don't feel like doing it, and I'm not gonna do it."

WENDY: [That] didn't really hit him until he was probably in junior high. And I've seen that with hormones before, you know, like even with ADHD, you'll see a change when the hormones hit. Then they sleep all the time. See, [when he was younger], he was awake all the time. He would stay up. I mean, I'd put him to bed, and then he'd be up sometimes in the middle of the night, you know, playing or reading or something. So he was, like, very active and didn't sleep very much at all and then, as soon as he hit puberty, it just switched. Then he became, like, sleeping in and not wanting to get up and so it really changed.

OPPOSITE Stills from Hisko Hulsing's animated sequence depicting the teenage Kurt experimenting with marijuana

TOP RIGHT AND BELOW Images from the Cobain family archive, with Kurt at the age of fifteen (top right) and sixteen (below)

KIM: He was also funny as hell. He would do goofy things to make someone laugh. He was a big goofball, you know.

WENDY: Like the day I came home from work. Kurt called me at work and said, "How do you know when spaghetti is

done?" And I said, "Well, throw a piece on the wall, and if it sticks, it's done." So I come home from work, and I looked up and a whole pot of spaghetti was hanging from my ceiling. At first I was, like, "What?" You know, I flipped out, and then I started laughing. I just thought it was hilarious. And we actually left it there. We thought it gave it a little character. And if you go there you can still see where it finally broke off.

KIM: There'd be very loud guitar and bad singing in his room. I don't know if it was the acoustics or he just didn't find his voice yet, but it was, like, the same chords over and over and over and over. And one time he did have me, like, sit in. Okay, we had this snare, and it was an old beat-up snare and then this cymbal hanging from a string on the ceiling in his bedroom. And we had this old toy box. It was wood, but it had this vinyl padding on it—that was the bass. He was, like,

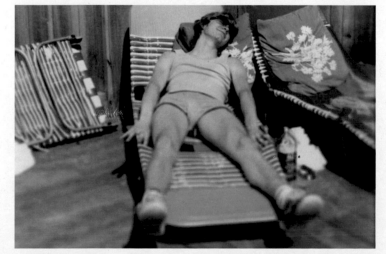

"Okay, all I want you to do is *boom-tap boom boom-tap*." And I go, "Okay." I'm just sitting there, like, *boom-tap*, and, oh my god, he went on for over an hour. I'm, like, "My arms hurt. I gotta stop." And he's, "No, you gotta keep going," and he pushed me and pushed me to do it.

WENDY: He was a writer, too, so there was a lot of quiet time that you didn't know what he was doing, but I just assumed that was what it was. So he wrote all the time. And he drew a lot and painted. And then I knew when he was playing music because it was loud. And he watched what was on MTV. He watched that a lot. Just to see what was new. He really liked watching the video clips. Getting ideas, like, I mean, I could see him thinking about, "Someday I'll be there. I'll be on MTV," you know? I didn't take it seriously. But I could see him really starting to pay attention to all of that. Very closely.

KIM: Kurt would take all these different albums and records and, you know, exercise tapes, whatever audio he could find, even if it was off the television. He'd make mix tapes. And it was just hilarious. I mean, it was such, like, it was a bunch of noise. I just really feel like that was what he felt like inside of his head.

WENDY: I mean, he could play any instrument. Like, a lot of kids in the neighborhood would join band and their parents would run right out [and] wouldn't rent. They would buy, like, a saxophone or a flute or whatever. And within two months the kid quit the class, and they would always send it over to Kurt, and he would start playing it, and they would go, "You can have that." So anything he picked up, he could play.

KIM: When I was a kid, I was kind of jealous of Kurt. But then as I grew up, I'm, like, "I'm so glad I never got that genius brain. I'm so thrilled that, like, I'm a normal human being, and I don't have that constant, constant thing going on in your brain of, 'You're not good enough.'" You have too much creativity in your brain that you have to release it somehow, and I think that was a big torment. I mean, I remember him just constantly having to do something. There's even lyrics in some of the songs, like, "I wish I was like you, easily amused." And, you know, he just wasn't. Day-to-day stuff just bored the crap out of him, and I think that's why he didn't do great in school. If they had the schools that they have today that kids go to, the alternative schools that focus on art and music and all that, he

KIM: I just don't think he knew where he was going. He ended up having to quit school because he had too many credits to make up, so, you know, he's, like, "I don't want to continue high school if I have to come back and do summer school and probably do a whole other senior year to make up for all the credits." And that's when my mom's, like, "Well, quit. But if you want to quit school, you have to get a job. You're gonna have to do something because you're not gonna just sleep all day and then go out and party with your friends all night and just live off of us, you know?"

would've been like, "Oh my god, okay, I found my place."

"He always needed something artistic."—WENDY

WENDY: He always needed something artistic. And school helped him in different genres of the arts, so he'd be all excited about clay. Or he'd be all excited about painting. And then when he got into painting, he loved it. Absolutely loved it. And then when he got into high school, he found oil painting, and he fell in love with that. He used to do water and then just acrylics. So he was always expanding with whatever thing that he was into. If it was painting, he always found new ways to expand that. And the same thing with music.

WENDY: When did I kick him out? That was tough-love days. Everybody was playing tough-love parenting. And I wish that phase never would have come in. [Later I] apologized to him a million times. He said, "Mom, please don't [apologize]. I was a badass. [I was] lazy, sleeping all day, living off of you, didn't finish school. What you did was exactly the right thing."

Conversation between Kurt Cobain and Buzz Osborne of the Melvins

KURT: [tape click] Hello? Hello?

BUZZ OSBORNE: You still there?

KURT: Yeah. I'm putting you on speaker phone now.

BUZZ: Okay. Are you recording this or writing it down?

KURT: Yeah, I'm recording and writing.

BUZZ: People don't realize where we really came from, you know? What an isolated hellhole it really is. I mean, if witch burnings had been, like, legal, we'd all be dead now. You know?

KURT: Fuck yeah. Did you ever see that movie *Over the Edge*?

BUZZ: Yeah!

KURT: I mean, god, that movie had such an effect on me.

KURT: I love that movie.

BUZZ: I always wanted to do that in front of you.

KURT: Me too. I, I tried, you know. I wanted to be a vandal, and I wanted to hold everyone captive in the school . . . Most of the teachers, god. The last couple of years of school in the mid-eighties, there was so much Reagan propaganda going on. This teacher would just go off on it everyday.

BUZZ: Burn the place to the fucking ground.

KURT: Yeah!

BUZZ: High school's such a worthless fucking nothing. God, what torture. You know?

KURT: No, I quit the last two months of school . . . I was so withdrawn by that time, and I was so anti-social that I was almost insane, you know? I felt so different and so crazy that people just left me alone.

OPPOSITE Politically themed art created by the teenage Kurt

DON: He lived with all kinds of different people. And he didn't have any place to go. We took him a couple times.

JENNY: We took him in because we heard he was living on the streets. But he wasn't. He didn't live by a bridge, either. I think everyone knows that. He went to that bridge to fish and play around, but he didn't live under a bridge. He liked comfort, and he just wouldn't do that. And so we just took him in, thinking that, you know, he didn't have anywhere to be. We found out later he was sleeping on a neighbor's couch, but we thought he was on the streets. Both of us, we were just really sad about that. So we talked about it with the kids and everything, and they said, "Well, let's get him back."

WENDY: So he went to live with, I don't even know who it was. I mean, I knew them. I knew him, the boy that he went to live with, and his mother called me, like, three weeks later and said, "Wendy, you know, I've got your son here living at my house." And I said, "Well, good luck, you know? All I wanted him to do was get a job and maybe get up before noon. So if you want to keep him in that condition, keep him. But if you need to kick him out, do it."

JENNY: The last time he came back, he was really into playing the guitar. And we could hear him, but we loved listening to it. And then drumming—drumming gets a little hard to listen to. Somebody said [Don] took his guitar away from him and

64

smashed it. No, I would've killed him. He just wouldn't do that. That was another thing that was some sort of rumor, but that was building up some sort of story about himself for people to feel sorry for him. And then, again, once he got here and there was discipline and things to do, he didn't want to do it. He just wanted to do what he wanted to do. [He] was around eighteen when last we had him.

KIM: I think he tried to get a job. My mom helped him with his résumé, and he got a job as a janitor. I mean, he was a janitor at the high school that he flunked out of, basically. And I think he got in trouble. I think he said he threw a computer out of the window or something. I don't know if that's true.

WENDY: He got a job, and he found this little dump [to live in]. I went down there, and I was, like, all my imagination couldn't have taken me to this place. I walked up on the step, and [it] fell through. There were walls—the inner part, you know, the two-by-four stringers, but no actual wall. He had turtles. This was actually his second place that he had lived in.

The first one, he and somebody—one of his friends—they only lasted about six weeks.

KIM: He poured concrete and built a terrarium for his turtles. He's only—I would say he's six blocks away from home and right behind our old grocery store.

WENDY: In between the first place he rented and that place, he moved back in [at home], and Krist would come over. And he's so tall, and he would come to the front door, and the front door had an archway, then the hallway arch, then the living room, another arch, the dining room, another arch into the kitchen, and then one more out the back door. And he always came through the front door. And it would be just, *bam bam bam*. He would be hitting his head. And I go, "You know, Krist, you can come to the back door, so there's only one to hit." It was cute. They were just really good friends. Krist was very quiet and very polite. Very nice. I liked him a lot. So [they actually had] a garage band, and they would play.

LOVE BUZZ

KRIST NOVOSELIC: I think I was eighteen- or nineteen-years-old, and Kurt was, like, seventeen [when we met]. He was this kid, and he was hanging out with some of those Aberdeen characters, but he liked punk rock music and so that piqued my interest. And he wasn't a mainstream person—he was a true counterculture person. I just thought he was pretty easygoing, and also he had a guitar and a guitar amp. And then I noticed what a good artist he was. He was working at the time at these resorts out in Ocean Shores, and he was a janitor out there. And again, he'd always have to, like, do some kind of art, usually defacing something. So, like, there was this flyer that he took from work about how to clean a razor clam, and then he changed it so that he put faces on it. It was really good—there's a razor clam, and then here comes a knife, and it's "No! No! Ahh . . . ahhh!" It's just this razor clam getting dismembered, and it was done really well, the way he changed it. So that was funny.

KIM: I wasn't around for a lot of that but, you know, when Kurt did find people that he could connect with, it was amazing. Like when he met Krist, and he used to follow the Melvins around like a little puppy, like, "Oh my god, I wanna be in their band! They're so great!" At that time they were much older, even though they're only a few years older. I think it helped him to kinda become who he was, like, "Okay, finally there's some people that I can connect with that also think the way I do."

OPPOSITE A still from Hisko Hulsing's animated sequence shows Kurt working on songs at Tracy's house
BELOW Krist Novoselic in Kurt Cobain: Montage of Heck

"And he'd come home kind of sad because he'd have this one girl that he was, like, crushing on and then she always had a jock boyfriend."—WENDY

KRIST: It happened organically. "Let's start a band because the Melvins [rehearsed] every day." So [Kurt] had a guitar amp and a guitar, and then I knew somebody where I could get a bass and a bass amp. Then we just needed a drummer. That's when the Melvins needed a new drummer and so Buzz [Osborne] approached me to see if I knew any drummers in Aberdeen. I said, "I know Dale Crover and Aaron Burckhard," and Buzz has stuck with Dale to this day. And Dale was, like, fifteen or sixteen, something like that. He was really young. So then Kurt and I went with Aaron and we started playing with Aaron, and he was just culturally different. [Aaron] made a racial slur in front of a black cop, and that was the deal-killer right there. That was, "We can't have this in our band. No."

TRACY MARANDER: [Kurt and I] started dating, I wanna say early summer, maybe of '87. The first time we met may have been at a party in Tacoma. I remember him in the kitchen with his pet rat on the shoulder. I talked to him a little bit about the rats, 'cause I had pet rats, just briefly talked to him.

WENDY: Kurt brought Tracy to the house, and I just loved her immediately. She came in, she had purple hair, she had this little skirt on that had little bells all the way around it. She was just sweet and just adored Kurt, and he was very respectful to her and loved her. And I was just really happy for him because she was a really, really neat person.

TOP Tracy Marander and Kurt Cobain in a photo taken by Krist's then-wife, Shelli Novoselic (now Shelli Hyrkas)

OPPOSITE Tracy Marander is interviewed for Kurt Cobain: Montage of Heck

TRACY: I think he had had one [girlfriend]. He had one not too long before that, maybe in high school. But I don't know how long they went out for. I can't remember.

WENDY: He would ask me questions about girls and try to figure out, you know, how to get one. And he'd come home kind of sad because he'd have this one girl that he was, like, crushing on and then she always had a jock boyfriend.

TRACY: I liked that he was funny. He made me laugh. He wasn't afraid to be goofy or silly. But mostly we just had a good time hanging out. I think he might have been a bit angry at the way he was treated at school. And angry with his mom and dad. I think it was not so much that it was hard for him to accept love but the fact that maybe he was afraid of it not working out and getting hurt.

KIM: Kurt wasn't your typical male. I mean, yeah, he was a guy, and he liked to do guy things, but the male macho thing, Kurt just . . . he loved women, so he wasn't condescending. And, also, he was around a lot of women. I mean, there were five women on my mom's side. He had four aunts and two uncles and one uncle that was gay, so . . . He wasn't one of those guys that was all about, "Oh, I gotta nail that chick." There were a lot of guys like that in Aberdeen.

TRACY: He was living in this tiny little house in Aberdeen that had just a couple of rooms and a stove. But no refrigerator. They kept their food in the ice chest on the porch. And it was him and Matt Lukin, and [there] might have been somebody else, I can't remember. But that's where they used to practice, too.

KRIST: It was, like, five times a week. Everyday. Or we'd get hung up because we'd have to go find Aaron, who was at the tavern. But we were super serious about it. We would have rehearsals that weren't ecstatic jams or whatever, and then we'd be kind of bummed out, like, "Oh, maybe we suck. We're not that good of a band." And then we'd have great rehearsals, and we'd go all far out and put songs together. Then we had our set list come together, and that was very satisfying. We were serious about being in a band.

TRACY: The first [Nirvana] show was at this house in Raymond at a party. They played in the living room; everyone was really drunk.

KRIST: Every night we liked to drink—just cheap wine mostly. Kurt was into, like, Ernest and Julio Gallo. We'd buy a gallon of it for, like, fifteen bucks or something. Kurt wasn't really into smoking pot. He was into wine and that kind of thing, and then he got into, you know, different kinds of drugs, but that's a whole different story. But I don't think we were, like, alcoholics. There were times when we didn't drink. And we never drank at practice. We were always sober and serious about that.

"He wasn't someone who'd come home and drink a beer or have a drink."—TRACY

TRACY: He wasn't someone who'd come home and drink a beer or have a drink. If we [went to a] show or party, he would drink, and he would drink hard alcohol— he didn't like beer—and then sometimes he would smoke pot at a party or something. And he smoked cigarettes a little bit, not like a big habit or anything. He didn't drink as much as Krist did.

WENDY: After Kurt moved out of the little house and really got into music with Krist, he moved up to Olympia and moved in with Tracy.

TRACY: At that point I was making all the money, even though that wasn't a lot. The rent was cheap and everything. It really was kinda hard for him to hold a job because, you know, they didn't know what nights they were gonna have practices and stuff, and then he really wanted to practice a lot more than the rest of the band did. I know he got annoyed with Krist sometimes because Krist couldn't practice because he had to work late. So that, well, annoyed Kurt, but he just ended up not having another job after that.

WENDY: If it wasn't for her, he would've starved to death.

TRACY: I supported him, yeah. He didn't get money from his mom or anything,

but I worked and I didn't mind. It was enough for two of us and all our pets. Sometimes he would wander around in Olympia, but usually he was writing songs, playing guitar, or creating art or different videos and cassette tape montages, writing stories.

KIM: He was always over at the house, even when he lived down the block with Tracy or in his little shack down the street. He would come home and have lunch or whatever. Mom would feed him if he needed to be fed, give him money when he needed money. It wasn't, you know, he wasn't abandoned.

TRACY: I know some people will say that I treated Kurt maternally, but I like to think it was more that I was trying to nurture him rather than take care of him. Trying to let him do his art and music and encourage him to get better at it, as opposed to trying to stifle it.

OPPOSITE Frames from a video of Kurt made by Krist Novoselic in Aberdeen

BELOW Tracy and Kurt's house in Olympia as it appeared during the time they lived there

FOLLOWING PAGES Kurt thumbs through his vinyl collection in this still from Hisko Hulsing's animation

OPPOSITE Video footage of Kurt filmed by Krist Novoselic

ABOVE Kurt creates montage art using anatomy images from medical books in this frame from Hisko Hulsing's animation

FOLLOWING PAGES An image from Hisko Hulsing's animated sequence showing domestic life for Kurt in the house he shared with Tracy

DON: He was sorta like me: lazy-like.

TRACY: We had a hand sink, and he'd do [dishes] sometimes—well, let me rephrase that. He did it at first sometimes, but then—this is the whiney part that comes in—he would complain that, if he would do dishes, it would soften the calluses on his fingertips that he needed to play guitar. But he couldn't wear rubber gloves because it made the dishes too slippery and they'd break.

KIM: It had to have been probably when he met Tracy that he got more into, like, nostalgia-type stuff. He really liked the toys of the '70s, and I think that the anatomy thing was just fascinating to him, you know? How did the body work? I think his fascination with human anatomy and what we can do and what

women can do, like, producing babies—that was just something in him.

TRACY: He had a lot of those Visible Man little figurines that he'd put together with anatomy and stuff, but I don't really know how much he was interested in it. I just know that he looked at it more like as an art thing. Maybe he was fascinated with the human body. But he would build those Visible Man things and then sometimes he'd get, like, a medical book with, like, really gross pictures in it of diseased parts of your body or something that he found in a thrift store. But I don't think he—I think that was just part of the art. I don't think it was a total fascination with it.

KRIST: He had an outlet. His creativity. And if you look at it, it's dark, and then

there's always some, like, mutilated body, some kind of organ, some kind of anatomy going on. In a lot of ways, it's very beautiful. I mean, it's well done. But something's not right. It's all off.

TRACY: He had a big collage on the wall with pictures of diseased vaginas and then, like, people or just random things that he made. I was just, like, "Oh, great," you know?

KIM: I think he found more beauty in what was underneath the skin. I think he found gross things beautiful. Because he was so precise with certain things or so infatuated with the human body and the way things work, he probably could have been a surgeon, if that would have been his passion. But I think he would have been more like Dr. Frankenstein,

you know, instead of a real doctor. He would have wanted to, like, "Oh, let's see if we can, you know, put the head of a donkey on, you know, this guy over here."

KRIST: It's all anatomy. Like, supermarket ad fliers come in the mail, and there's all that meat. He'd cut that out, you know, and just make these collages. I don't know. The id is driving him, like, underneath the surface. It's anatomy, or it's just meat.

TRACY: A lot of his art was pretty dark, you know, and maybe that's just the things he thought of. I know he always said that he had really violent dreams a lot. People would be breaking into his house trying to kill him, and he'd have to stab them to get away from them or stab

OPPOSITE AND TOP Kurt works on art projects in a Hisko Hulsing animated sequence

them to protect his family or friends. I don't know what that was about, but maybe that was part of it.

KIM: When he was living with Tracy in Olympia, there was a music scene there, and he met other people. I mean, there was K Records and [The] Evergreen [State College] radio station, and there were a lot of people into music there. There's a lot more access to, you know, other people that were into music and into kind of underground type music, and I think that that was something that just helped him.

KRIST: We had recorded a demo with Jack Endino at Reciprocal Studios in, like, 1988, probably. We made the demo, and Jack liked it, and he gave a copy to Jonathan [Poneman] at Sub Pop. Then Jonathan was starting this label and was recruiting bands, and it was, "Hey, you wanna do a single?" Sub Pop was doing a series of singles, only a thousand copies or something like that, and we were, like, "Absolutely!" So things were happening.

TRACY: Once Sub Pop called, and they wanted to put them on the label, he was just so ecstatic. He listened to the answering machine message, like, twenty times just to hear it over and over again.

KRIST: I remember the first review Nirvana ever got was for the "Love Buzz" / "Big Cheese" single. It was in this hip magazine out of Michigan, and they gave us a bad review. They said it was like Lynyrd Skynyrd but without the flares. Kurt was really hurt by that. And I said, "Don't worry about it. They're just scenesters. They're hipsters. Screw them." And, you know, I didn't feel good about it either. But he took it hard.

JENNY: He would get into stressful situations where most people will get a headache, but he would get stomach problems. And that kind of followed him for a long time because he was never quite as secure or as confident as he wanted to be.

TRACY: He'd throw up a lot of times before his shows. He would say it wasn't nervousness, but I don't know. I know he had the whole separate stomach issue/food thing going on. But pretty much every time he threw up was before a show.

KRIST: Kurt hated being humiliated. He hated it. He *hated* it. If he ever thought he was being humiliated, then you'd see

the rage come out. And so he was also very careful and stubborn about the way the art and the work was presented, because he didn't want to be humiliated. I could be humiliated—I humiliate myself and whatever—but not Kurt, no.

KIM: Kurt took it to a whole other level, you know? When he was shamed, he really felt it. It was hard for him to let go.

KRIST: He had a lot of feelings. He could be sweet, but he could be vicious, too. I guess there was a dichotomy there: He could be really bland and unamused, or he could be very intense. Kurt was an artist. He always had to express himself—he never had, like, idle hands, you know? He wasn't lazy. He'd never not get out of bed, but he'd never clean his kitchen or clean his house. He just wasn't interested in that. He'd always be drawing or making sculptures or making music. He was always compelled to express himself somehow.

TRACY: I think when people refer to him being lazy it's because he didn't work, and eventually he didn't want to clean the house anymore and left that to me. But, as far as the music went, even his art, he pursued that. He sent the copies of their tape to the record companies, trying to get [signed], and then [he tried] to get shows booked and to get people to pay attention to him. And [he was] practicing to get better. Even when he watched TV—some people might just sit there for a few hours and zone out. He would be playing guitar and just kind of doodling and doodling, and eventually he [would come] up with a song and then [record] it. Or he'd write something in a journal. He did want success. He was ambitious. He didn't want to play in a bar band. He wanted to become successful. Not Guns N' Roses successful, but more [like] R.E.M. [or] the Pixies. He

BELOW A tape featuring Kurt's artwork for an early iteration of the band, plus contact information for the benefit of interested record companies

OPPOSITE A page from Kurt's private journals that highlights his apparent fear of humiliation

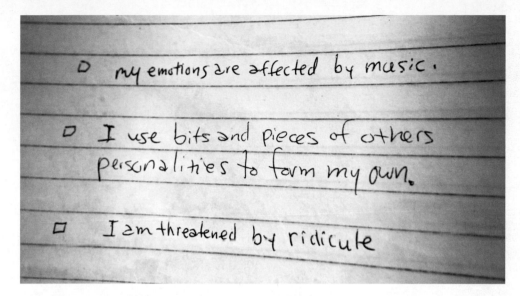

□ my emotions are affected by music.

□ I use bits and pieces of others personalities to form my own.

□ I am threatened by ridicule

loved the Pixies. He just didn't want to become a super-huge megastar.

KRIST: Kurt made these press kits, and he put all these tapes together, and he mailed them to Touch and Go [Records]. He was really ambitious when we were looking for a record deal. And in 1991 he wanted to have billboards. He wanted to be promoted. So he was very confident, and he was the most ambitious person.

TRACY: I don't know if I'd call him a genius, but he seemed to have a knack for writing songs that people liked. Whether it was the more rough stuff on *Bleach* or the more produced stuff on *Nevermind*, he just seemed to have a good knack for writing it. And you know, Krist contributed to some of that, too, the bass lines and whatnot, and Dave Grohl later on.

KRIST: See, there's total confidence. We would just try to be ecstatic. We were really serious about the music—we had to feel the music. We loved music, and we weren't dogmatic punks. There was a lot of ideology and dogma with punk rock back then, and we just didn't feel that way at all. We still liked Black Sabbath

"Kurt hated being humiliated."—KRIST

and Led Zeppelin and hard rock music. And the punk rock music was great, too. I mean, it was all just music, and that's how we envisioned the band, just to make this kind of music. We just had to feel the music and especially Kurt. It had to be that way for him because he was so emotive. That's why the music is so enduring to this day. People can feel it.

WENDY: I didn't know that he had tried heroin. [Ed: Kurt wrote in a journal that in 1987 he tried heroin for the first time in Aberdeen and then about ten more times between then and 1990.] Because in Aberdeen . . . that really surprises me.

TRACY: See, he never told me that. He totally had kept that from me. I didn't find out. I had so many people who told me that, but, at the time, I did not know at all. Because I would totally talk to him about that. In fact, he used to make fun of some of the people in Seattle that were using that. Say it was really stupid. So I don't know if he wanted to fit in with them or just . . . I don't know.

"We thought it was Crohn's disease, ulcers, you know, everything."—WENDY

TOP Kurt creates a private audio recording in a scene from a Hisko Hulsing animated sequence

OPPOSITE Kurt plays an acoustic guitar in this frame from a Hisko Hulsing animated sequence

WENDY: I think that he had tried it because of his stomach problems. Well, he was lactose intolerant, and he ate tons of ice cream. I mean, it's really a bad thing when you're lactose intolerant. He did go to many doctors that misdiagnosed him. We thought it was Crohn's disease, ulcers, you know, everything. And I think [because of the pain] that he just tried a drug that just fucked him up for his life. It was a drug that was somewhere where it was available to him at some point, and he tried it. And he just—I guess the euphoria

is just so intoxicating. It's like a feeling that you've never felt before in your life. And that's why it's so dangerous. I mean, one time and you can be hooked. And that's what happened.

TRACY: Kurt would get stomach aches alot. You know, he'd be feeling fine and then get out of the car and just be like, "I gotta throw up." I know he went to the doctor once or twice, but it didn't really work.

KRIST: He started dabbling in heroin in . . . I think it was '90, early '91. He got associated with some of these Seattle people who were into the smack scene,

NIRVANA

© ℗ 1989 the end of music (BMI) 102
NIRVANA - BLEACH

A	Noise Reduction	B	Noise Reduction
	EQ High(CrO2): 70μs		EQ High(CrO2): 70μs
BLEW		Negative Creep	
Floyd the barber		Scoff	
About a girl		Swap meat	
School		mr moustache	
Love Buzz		Sifting	
Paper cuts			
NIRVANA		BLEACH	

"He got associated with some of these Seattle people who were into the smack scene, and so then he was dabbling in it."—KRIST

and so then he was dabbling in it. And then he got money, and then he could buy all that he wanted. And so I think that was a big deal, right there. That took a physical toll on him.

TRACY: I can't really say exactly why we broke up. I just know that we were fighting more, and he was staying away from the house more. And first he said he wanted to get separate places to live but still be boyfriend and girlfriend. And then eventually I'd come home, and he wouldn't be there. And, it turns out, people tell me he was staying at Tobi's [Bikini Kill drummer Tobi Vail] apartment all the time. Then I asked him if he was sleeping with Tobi, and he said, "No," and I asked him a few more times, and he kept saying "No." And then eventually I moved out, and I was pissed, too, because he was supposed to help me pack everything into the truck, and he didn't come home that day to help. It turned out later he told me that he was sleeping with Tobi, but he didn't want to hurt my feelings, so that's why he didn't tell me.

TOP LEFT Kurt drew many different logos for the band, including this one that features a guitar reminiscent of the model he would come to be associated with, the Fender Jaguar

ABOVE Homemade tapes from Kurt's archive, including his personal recording of Nirvana's first album, Bleach

OPPOSITE TOP Illustration of sick man by Kurt

OPPOSITE BOTTOM A page from one of Kurt's journals that seems to confirm that he took heroin as early as 1987

I tried heroine the first time in
1987 in aberdeen and proceeded to
to use it about 10 more times from
87 to 90.

For five years every single day
an ongoing stomach ailment had
literally taken me to the point
of wanting to kill myself.

The pain became even more
severe due to lack of a proper

MAY women rule the world.

KIM: I think that, you know, he had been around all these different types of women his whole life, and he was with Tracy—a very sweet, sensitive, great person—but there's no way she could've handled the explosion of what happened. And where he was going . . . He knew his drug addiction was a problem, and he didn't want to drag her into that.

WENDY: He called me to wish me a happy birthday, and then he got serious, and he said, "I've got something really serious to tell you. I have to break up with Tracy." I was just floored. I go, "What? Oh my god, Kurt. It's gonna break her heart." He goes, "I know. I just know it's the best for her, Mom. This

OPPOSITE Kurt and Tracy together in a photo taken by Shelli Hyrkas

TOP A page from one of Kurt's journals as it appears in the documentary

"He knew his drug addiction was a problem, and he didn't want to drag her into that."—KIM

[is] my first really big huge European tour, and it's gnarly, and it's bad, and it's hard, and she deserves better than this." And he just knew that what she wanted wasn't gonna be this lifestyle. I mean, that's how much he loved her. And I said, "Well, that's sweet of you, and you know, I'm sad, and I love her."

TRACY: I haven't heard that. That's a nice sentiment, I guess.

SERVE THE SERVANTS

COURTNEY LOVE: "Oh, fuck, yeah. He wanted to be the biggest rock star in the world. We were both competing with each other, you know, but they were making *Nevermind*. I heard the Butch Vig demos. I knew they were going to be pretty goddamn big. I thought maybe a quarter million, half a million. [Then] I heard "Smells Like Teen Spirit" was the number one most requested song on K-Rock.

KRIST: "Smells Like Teen Spirit—" I wasn't really impressed with it when we first started it. There were other songs that I thought were way better, like "In Bloom." We started working on "In Bloom," and it sounded like a Bad Brains song. We'd kick that around, and then Kurt took it home and rearranged it. He called me on the phone, and he was, like, "Check this out!" And he started doing "In Bloom." And I'm, like, "That's great! Sounds cool." We rehearsed it, and I started busting out some bass lines, and the song just came together. And melodic songs like "On a Plain," those were always my favorites because I like doing the melodies. I could always do some kind of Paul McCartney bass or something. But "Smells Like Teen Spirit," Kurt came home with that riff and that song. We were playing it big, and we just brought it back down again. After a while, that's what we were doing. We were into these dynamics. It was one of our tricks in our bag of tricks.

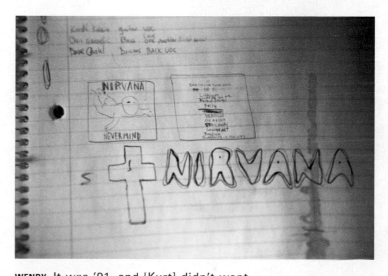

WENDY: It was '91, and [Kurt] didn't want to have an apartment anymore to pay for because he was on tour so much, so he asked me if he could come home. I said, "Of course." And so he comes home, and he's there three days, it's a Sunday morning, and I'm in the bathroom. [He] knocks very quietly on the door, and he goes, "Mom?" And I go, "Yeah?" And he goes, "I have a tape." I open the door, and he's standing there with this tape in his hand, and I go, "What's that?" And he goes, "It's the master cut to my new album." And he goes, "Can I put it in the stereo?" and I go, "Yeah, and turn it up, up, up," 'cause I listen to music really loud. So I kept putting my makeup on, and I'm like, "Holy shit!" I just run out of the bathroom. I mean, it took two or three notes, and I'm out of the bathroom. And he's just sitting at the end of the sofa, and [he has] that kind of a smirk, like he's the cat-that-ate-the-canary look.

OPPOSITE Kurt records at Hilversum Studios in the Netherlands [photo by Michel Linssen]

TOP A page from Kurt's journals featuring an early sketch of what would become the iconic cover for the Nevermind *album*

And I look at him and I go, "Oh my god, oh my god," I'm just screaming at him, and I'm pounding on his shoulder with my finger going, "Do you know what you've done?" He went, "*Pfft*. You're just my mom." And I almost started crying. I mean, not from happiness—from fear. It was fear. And I just went, "This is going to change everything in music." And I said, "You better buckle up, 'cause you are not ready for this."

KRIST: The mainstream came to us, and all of a sudden there was an impact on culture. And if you look at the rock bands that were popular just before Nevermind, the hair metal bands, they had flowery hair and a lot of makeup. They had a very feminine look, but they

had this macho bravado, they're studs out there ready to take on the chicks. And then Nirvana comes out and our "grunge revolution" happens, alternative music. And then, the aesthetic, it shifts and so we have like flannel shirts, facial hair, and ripped jeans, but then we're all sensitive, like we have our feminine side too.

KIM: Everybody says that was Kurt's main goal: to become famous and be a rock star. I don't think so. I didn't feel that from him. It was, "I can do this. I really like it," and then "Oh, shit." You know? Like, now everybody's listening to it. He contradicted himself constantly. I want to do this, but I don't want to do this. I love to make music, and I want the

OPPOSITE, TOP, AND FOLLOWING PAGES Images from the Nevermind *album cover shoot [photos by Kirk Weddle]*

Kurt talks to the press at the height of Nirvana's fame.

ABOVE *Video footage of Nirvana playing at the Paradiso in Amsterdam, 1991*

OPPOSITE *Nirvana at the Astoria, London, in October 1990 [photo by Matt Anker]*

INTERVIEWER: You guys don't like explaining anything to do with your music. What's the problem with going on camera and just—

KURT: There's nothing to be said, it's all in the music, man. It's all in the music. It's all in the meat!

INTERVIEWER: You don't, you don't think that people that are fans of you would like to hear what, what you had in mind maybe? Or what you were—

KURT: I'd rather hear what they have, have in mind, you know? Like, how they interpret it.

whole world to hear it, but I don't want the praise from it.

KRIST: Well, Kurt wanted the band promoted on billboards. He wanted all this, you know, promotion. We signed with DGC, and they print up 50,000 copies of *Nevermind*, which is supposed to last us a couple years. And then it goes ballistic. You can't buy *Nevermind* for, like, a month, which just adds to the mystique. People go to the record store and wanna buy this record. "We don't have it." But again, it might just be that dichotomy of being underground—Kurt could be really withdrawn and out of the mainstream, but then he wanted to be famous.

COURTNEY: [He went] up to the top of the Wishkah hill, saying to the gods, "I'm going to become the biggest rock star in the world and kill myself when I'm twenty-seven." Those were his words. He said that. You know, he told me. He said that out loud. You know, so, I mean, I didn't believe any of this shit. I thought, "These are mythologies that we're creating for ourselves just like Bob Dylan and his whole Woody Guthrie bullshit." You know, "I lived on trains." You're a middle-class, nice Jewish boy from Duluth. You know what I mean? So he was sophisticated enough to know that you can lie to the media about your creation story, and it could be whatever you want.

WENDY: During interviews he would downplay how good he was. And that was his goal—to be as good as he could be and maybe there was a little bit of embarrassment to that. Maybe he just felt praise was hard to take so he would downplay it all the time. But his goal was to get to as perfect as he could: write as well as he could, sing as well as he could, play as well as he could. And then when it all came together, he

"Kurt wanted to build a home because his home and his family fell apart."—KRIST

got embarrassed. And he was kind of like that all the way through his life . . . I would see that happen to him in school. They'd be, like "Oh, Kurt, that's so good. How do you do that?" And he would be, like, "Oh, well, anybody can do that" . . . He didn't know how to handle that. And it continued in a lot of interviews that he did.

KRIST: Each individual is gonna deal with it the way they're gonna deal with it. It was kind of traumatic to be famous all of a sudden, especially coming from complete obscurity and then being the number one band in the world. So I did things like withdraw, drink. But I'm lucky—I had beer and wine. Kurt had heroin, which takes a bigger, faster toll. Beer and wine will take a toll, but I could always stop drinking and, like, go running. That was one of my things. Maybe I don't have that addictive personality. I could abuse alcohol, I can binge or whatever. But it never took over. It seemed like the heroin could take over with Kurt. It would just dominate his life, and that's a powerful drug.

COURTNEY: I had already done heroin, beat the thing, had a rule. I loved it still, but I didn't have a fantasy that he had. He had a fantasy. His fantasy was, "I'm going to get to three million dollars . . ."—maybe it was only a million, but I think it was three—"I'm going to get to three million dollars, and then I'm going to be a junkie." Those are his words.

KRIST: Kurt wanted to build a home because his home and his family fell apart. So then he did it. When he and Courtney came together, he just

Transcript from Kurt and Courtney's home videos

COURTNEY: Girls don't masturbate over their teen idols.

KURT: They don't?

COURTNEY: No, they make up more intricate, schematic plans. Girls are a lot more complex than boys. You don't know what girls do to each other.

KURT: Yes, I do.

COURTNEY: No, you don't.

KURT: They're vicious.

COURTNEY: I mean, it's, like, you can know about crafty girls like all you want, but I wouldn't let you go on tour with crafty girls because, fucking, doesn't fucking matter, man. They, they . . . they diss me. They diss me all the time . . . but I can't, and I know it's not even like I can't trust you, it's just you can't trust men in general, even, even if they're "new men" and, and they're you. Even if they're like you, you still can't trust them.

KURT: I understand what you're trying to say, but I don't agree.

COURTNEY: You just, you just—

KURT: I am the "new man." I'm a man for the '90s. I'm Ward Cleaver, 1992.

COURTNEY: And then, you being you, you'd be all sensitive, and you'd go, "How are we going to tell Courtney?"

KURT: [Chuckles]

COURTNEY: Meanwhile, I've ruined my career, ruined my life, become the most hated woman in America, and become 200 pounds so I can—

KURT: But you were already the most hated woman in America.

COURTNEY: What?

KURT: You and Roseanne Barr are tied for being the most hated woman in America.

COURTNEY: Okay, I married Bobby Sherman, I'm the most hated woman, ruined my body, not play at the Reading Festival this year when I could've kicked your ass. Just—

KURT: You could. You should still play the Reading Festival.

COURTNEY: Oh, yeah. So I should just play the Reading Festival.

KURT: Dive into the crowd

COURTNEY: Right, that's right.

KURT: Shoot off a gun, light yourself on fire . . .

COURTNEY: Mhm. Everyone wants to see this—

KURT: . . . give the bird.

COURTNEY: . . . and this is only half of it. The rest is yet to come.

OPPOSITE Kurt and Courtney in Europe, 1991

wanted to build a home with her. And part of that home was doing drugs. And when he started doing heroin was when he and I started to move apart. But Courtney didn't turn Kurt onto heroin—he was already experienced with it. So that's not her fault. And then whatever her issues are—I'm not judging anybody—but that's just a fact that they got together, and that was part of their relationship.

COURTNEY: We were perfect together. We just had so much synchronicity and were soulmates, and we were awesome. We just were and we loved each other madly and we could finish each other's sentences and he would talk and it would be like fairy dust was coming out of his mouth and he was just a beautiful soul. So I've definitely been in love again

TOP Wendy with Kurt and Courtney at their wedding shower, 1992

OPPOSITE B-roll footage from the "Come As You Are" video shoot

other than him, but I've never remarried I think out of just . . . I don't know if anyone could top that feeling.

WENDY: It was 1991. I'd gotten a phone call from Kurt. He'd just gotten back from London. And he says, "Hey, Mom, this is Kurt." He always told me that it was him, which I thought was funny. And he goes, "Mom, I got something to tell you." And I go, "What?" And he goes, "I'm getting married." And it was just, like, kind of yelled and [Courtney] said in the background, "Kurt! You can't tell your mom something like that over the telephone. You need to go to her house and tell her, right?" And he goes, "Oh . . ." And I said, "Do I know her?" And he goes, "No." And I said, "Well, what's she like?" And he said, "Crazy." And I said, "Really?" And I go,

"He knew he needed a strong person in his life that could take charge when he couldn't."—WENDY

"Crazier than me?" And he goes, "Oh, yeah." So, he kind of told me a little bit about her, and I just got the impression that she was going to steam-roll right over me.

KIM: [Courtney's] a bulldozing, strong, take-charge woman. [She] would take over anything he didn't want to deal with. She's abrasive. She's loud.

WENDY: I think that he knew he had to nail her down to survive this. I really do. He knew he needed a strong person in his life that could take charge when he couldn't.

COURTNEY: [It was perceived that I was] the aggressor, and he was meek. I'm not going to sit here and tell you he was a fucking lumberjack who threw me against the wall and raped me, but he was definitely an alpha male sexual person. He just didn't come off that way in interviews, and I have to rescue his masculinity from the shadows. It's like, he wasn't an effeminate person. He just wasn't. You can't put together a band, keep a band together, write those fucking songs, keep all that shit in your head, and go out and perform the way that he did from 1987 to 1994 if you're a fucking Walter Mitty. You've got to be like a hunter. You've got to really want it and be a sharp shooter.

KIM: [Courtney's] in your face. And Kurt was the complete opposite of that. But he also didn't put up with her bullshit, and she didn't put up with his. I mean they, you know, there were certain dynamics that I think worked, and there were certain dynamics that didn't.

COURTNEY: We were in Seattle and we went down to Nordstrom and he bought me a bunch of Chanel makeup and I was so happy. We were sitting on the street. I'd never had all this Chanel makeup in my life. That was the day we bought my wedding ring, and it was just this simple rose-gold ruby. I mean, it was literally $1,400 dollars, and we were ecstatic about it. [We also bought a] $64,000 dollar Lexus [that] made us both uncomfortable. I think we got made fun of for it so we returned it. But I think a little more money spread out a little in a better lifestyle would've been educational and very, very helpful. It might've saved him.

WENDY: From what he told me, they had kind of gone in hiding for a week or so together, and she wanted to get married, and he was, like, "Mmm, well, maybe," or something like that. And so they were walking down the street and he said that a bird had fallen onto the sidewalk from a tree that was hanging over the sidewalk. A baby bird . . . He picked it up and put it in his hand, and it didn't look like it was gonna survive, and he said, "All right, I'll make you a deal. If this baby bird flies out of my hands, I'll marry you, and if it doesn't, I won't." And it flew out of his hands. But there was a contingency that he put there with it. Yeah, he just said, "I want you to have my baby." And she agreed to it, but I don't think that she was thinking that he would actually make her do that. And I said, "So, she's gonna have the baby before you get married then? Or what? How's this gonna work?"

COURTNEY: I don't think I would be capable of marrying and bearing the child of somebody I wasn't fully in love with. It's not in my DNA to do that.

KIM: When Kurt and Courtney got together, it was—I don't know. He was on tour a lot and so I never really saw him anyway, but they were kind of isolating themselves because they were the only ones that were doing drugs together so, you know, there wasn't, it wasn't like a group family thing, and that's what they were kind of doing for pretty much their entire relationship.

KRIST: I think Courtney pushed him to get out there because she was really ambitious. [It was] good for the band because we did want go out there and go on tour, but tours are demanding and you need to look good and be in good shape . . .

COURTNEY: Okay. So we had gone to Amsterdam on tour, Nirvana's tour, and it's a hashish district; it's not a heroin district. But in Zurich they have Needle Park, so we assumed there would be heroin in this hashish district. There wasn't. But we found this busker and [he] was able to lead us somewhere deep into Amsterdam to get some heroin, and it was really good heroin. It was, like, as Keith Richards once quoted Muddy Waters, "If god made something better, he kept it for himself." [Later] Nirvana's on tour in England, and I'm on tour [in Amsterdam]. I'm working. And Kurt's stomach is killing him, and he wants heroin really bad. And they get to Glasgow or Edinburgh, one of the two, and Kurt's walking around, like, asking punters, but he's Kurt Cobain and he can't do it. He's getting fucking mobbed. So I'm in Amsterdam. He's, like, "Can you find our busker?" Because I'm coming to London. At that point I had been on the cover of *Melody Maker* and *NME*, and Kurt had said that thing on [the British

TV show] *The Word* about me being the greatest fuck in the world and, you know, all this stuff. And I'm, like, "Yeah, but that means I'm smuggling heroin. If I get caught, I'm going to be in jail for a really long time." "Put it in your shoe," he said. Not the most genius idea. So I find the busker miraculously. He leads me to the heroin. (This is so not romantic, by the way.) I find the heroin, I get the heroin, and I have it on the plane with me, and I am sweating bullets. I'm going to jail. Have you ever seen *Midnight Express*? Because I have, okay? And I'm, like, I'm going to be sweltering it out in [jail at] Wormwood Scrubs for the rest of my days and then I'll get deported, and I'll end up in Arizona in some crazy isolation tank, and everyone will cheer because I'm a villain. I was already a rock villainess.

So I land, and I stick the [heroin] balloons in a [bottle of] liquid foundation. I land, and I just turn my sociopath button up, you know. They take me to the side, they go through all my stuff, they bend me over, a cavity search. And they never found it, which is the insane part. So I get that heroin through Heathrow. I get to [Kurt's] door, and he's, like, "Did you get it?" I'm, like, "Yes, I got it, but they made me bend over." He's, like, "God, I love you. You would do that for me? Will you marry me?" That's the story. It's so not romantic. There it is. It's the truth, and it's the true story. And I'm, like, "Yeah, I'll marry you but not because you think I'm your drug mule." He's, like, "No, but no one else would do that for me." And I'm, like, "You're right, that's true." I must have loved him a lot.

BELOW Kurt onstage at the Reading Festival [photo by Charles Peterson]

OPPOSITE A fragment of a smashed up guitar from Kurt's archive featuring lyrics from "Frances Farmer Will Have Her Revenge on Seattle"

Transcript from Kurt and Courtney's home videos

KURT: At the height of their drug abuse. Damn, if I wasn't so needle sick, I'd be on tour with Guns N' Roses right now. Me and Axl would be whooping it up, snake dancing across speakers.

COURTNEY: Snake dancing across the stage together singing Nazareth's songs.

KURT: But I'm too goddamn needle sick, man.

COURTNEY: Are you fucked up, baby?

COURTNEY: [Singing] You will see, you and me, Kurt, please, be with me. I want to be your girlfriend, I want to be your girlfriend. Let me just be your girlfriend. Let me just be your girlfriend . . . well I put it in my anus, and it kind of was heinous, but I put it in my belly, and it kind of was smelly. And I want to be your girlfriend. I want to be your girlfriend. I want to ride your bratmobile, baby. I want to know how you really feel, yeah. I want to ride in your bratmobile. I want to shoot up in your bratmobile, 'cause you put it in my belly, and I feel sexy.

KURT: I feel insane. Put it in my vein.

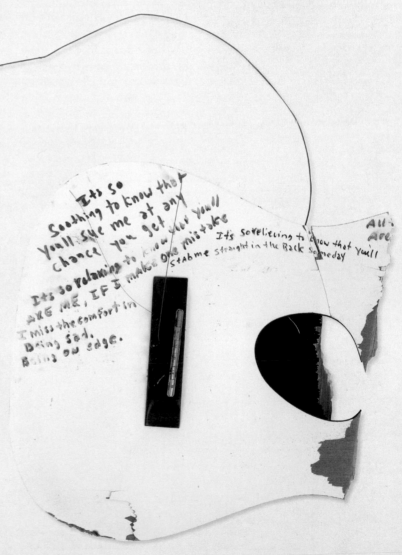

"And he was, like, 'Whatever. But if you ever, ever *think* about doing heroin, I'll get a gun, and I'll fucking kill you.'"—KIM

KRIST: We recorded *Nevermind*, and after *Nevermind* was done, he moved on. I told him not to do heroin, and he didn't listen, you know? I told him not to get married, but he wouldn't listen. Maybe he didn't like that advice and so, you know, he was doing his thing. So we'd hang out, I'd go over to his house and we'd watch some TV, talk or whatever, but not as much as we used to. And then we'd go to rehearsal, and that was what kept the band together, because we really liked playing together, and we could do things so fast. Dave and Kurt and I, we could write songs in minutes just outta jams. Or Kurt would have a song, and he'd bust a riff out, and it wouldn't take very long to arrange it. We just knew what to do, and we'd be happy. At rehearsals we'd be happy because we'd be playing, and that's kind of what kept us together—just making the music.

OPPOSITE Kurt being wheeled onstage at the Reading Festival, August 30, 1992 [photo by Charles Peterson]

BELOW Kurt onstage at the Reading Festival [photo by Charles Peterson]

FOLLOWING PAGES Animation imagery created by Stefan Nadelman and based on personal art from Kurt's archive

KIM: [Kurt] was trying to get cleaned, and he came home to kinda detox and that's what he would do sometimes. And so this was in '91. And we're sitting there and he's, like, "I know you've done pot, and I know you've done coke." And I'm, like, "No, I haven't done coke. I've never done it." He's, like, "Ah, you will." And I'm, like, "No, I won't!" We had this whole yes-you-will, no-I-won't back-and-forth for, like, five minutes. And he was, like, "Whatever. But if you ever, ever *think* about doing heroin, I'll get a gun, and I'll fucking kill you." He's, like, "I'll just kill you. Because you better just stay the fuck away from that shit. It's the most evil crap in the world." And I'm just, like, "Don't worry." Of course, it was hypocritical, but it was him again, protecting his sister. He didn't want to be a junkie. He didn't want to be doing heroin and dealing with addiction. He didn't want that. And he told me. I'm, like, "What is it like? What does it do to you? What is so horrible about it?" He's, like, "What's so horrible about it is it's the most wonderful thing in the world. It takes away everything for that moment."

KRIST: There was just this dark, dark vibe. There were times when he was in rehab that it got so bad. Or he'd be holed up in some hotel, and there'd have to be somebody there to just watch him, and he'd go on this smack binge. And that took a toll on the band because Dave and I aren't into heroin. I've never seen heroin before. I've never done heroin. So there you have it.

COURTNEY: Then we got married in February of '92.

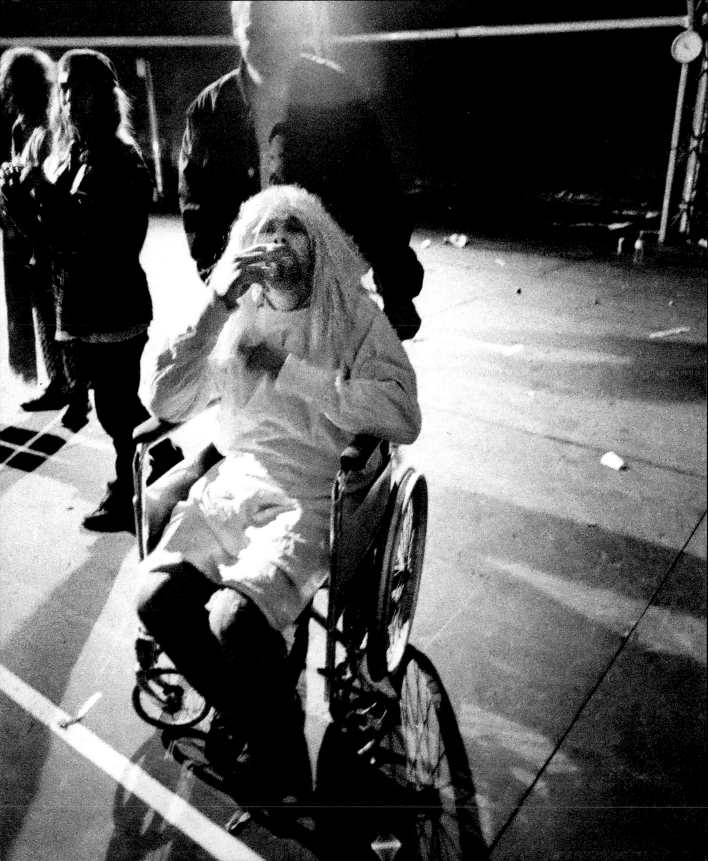

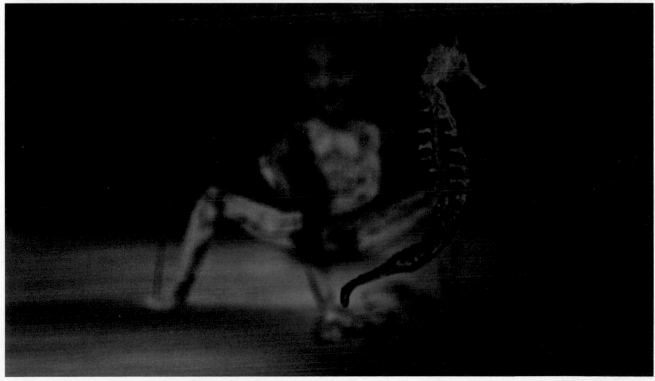

"[O]ne of my biggest regrets is not having—even though they'd be fucked up and not have a dad—is not having another child with Kurt."—COURTNEY

the MALe Seahorse carries the children

and gives them Birth.

WENDY: She was pregnant before they got married.

COURTNEY: Oh, god, yes. Yes, we wanted to have a baby, and I conceived Frances in December. So, I was pregnant when I got married, yes. So, I know the day. I remember the actual sex that conceived her. You know, you have children, and there is that kind of sex you have that is baby-making sex; it's just magical sex. I mean, sex is one of the great pleasures that we as humans are afforded and that we can just get naturally and, you know, one of my biggest regrets is not having—even though they'd be fucked up and not have a dad—is not having another child with Kurt. I really wish that we had made two babies because we made a good baby with the first one. We

were still in our twenties. I was fertile Myrtle, so, you know . . .

WENDY: I would get phone calls from Courtney, "Kurt's overdosed," and, "He's okay," and, you know, it was horrible. And knowing that a little baby was on its way, it just broke my heart.

COURTNEY: I assured him that I was built like an ox and could carry this pregnancy to term and not have any problems. But, you know, I was a young woman. The pregnancy isn't the problem. It's the being around a junkie while I'm pregnant when I'm a junkie, too, and I know that the minute that baby's out I'm going to go shoot up in celebratory fashion. You know what I mean? Like, that was our lifestyle.

TOP, OPPOSITE, AND FOLLOWING PAGES Birth-themed imagery created by Stefan Nadelman, based on Kurt's personal art

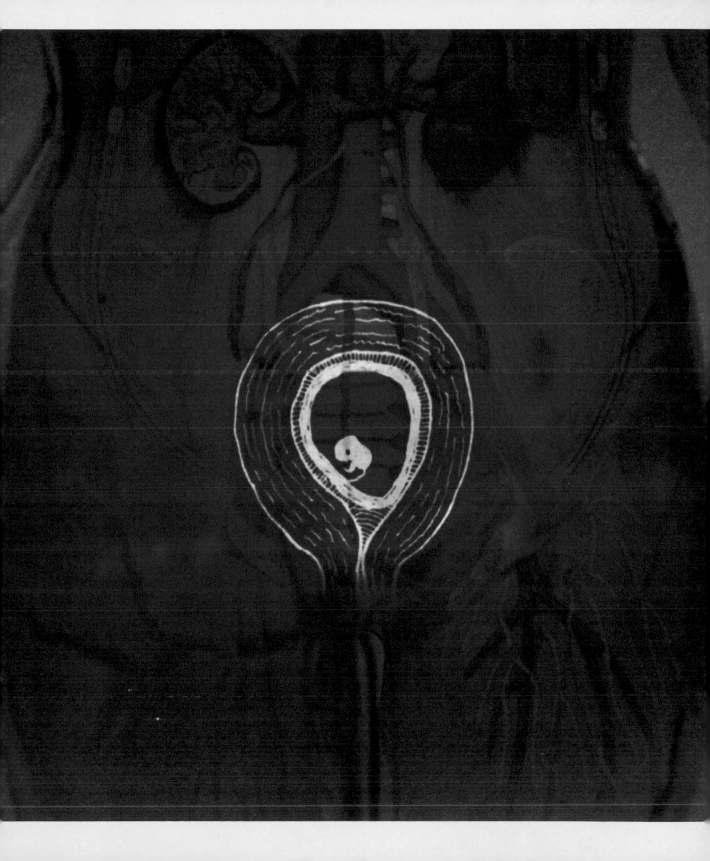

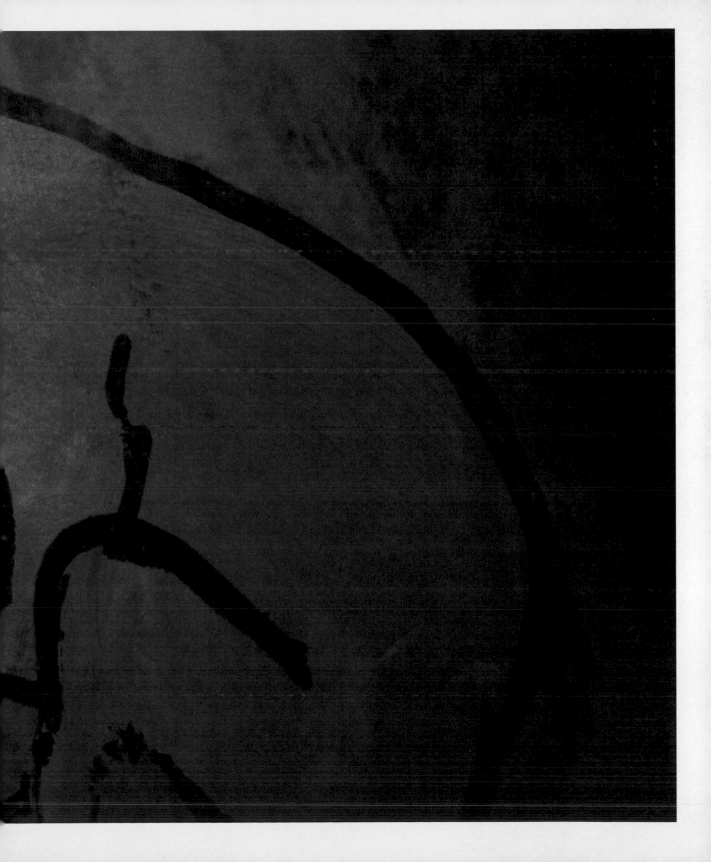

ANEURYSM

KRIST: Kurt was under a lot of pressure at that time, and once the band was huge and he had, like, addiction issues, that didn't help. When Nirvana broke big, because it was Kurt who was up there—he was singing, he was writing the music, he was playing the guitar—that was a lot of pressure on him. And, like, touring was a lot of pressure on him because he would give so much. You watch those performances, and it would just wear him out.

"It was just really hard to be famous all of a sudden."—KRIST

COURTNEY: I had wanted to be famous my whole life, as did he, but he hadn't thought out any of it. I thought out that part. I had a look. I had a hairdo. I had a style. And so did he, but that was accidental. Like, I tried to explain to him what that meant. I'm, like, "Okay, you have a double page in the *New York Times* in the fashion section. You're a fashion icon." He was, like, "What?" I'm, like, "Yeah. Anything you wear is going to get copied. This is big news." And he just was, like, "This is weird." He goes, "Is the *New York Times* really that important?" I'm, like, "The *New York Times* is what's called the paper of record, so if you get, for instance,

creamed in the *New York Times*, you might want to look at your work because you probably might've sucked. I mean, that doesn't apply to everything, but the *New York Times* is important."

KRIST: It was just really hard to be famous all of a sudden. It was great in a lot of ways. And I'm not complaining. I bought a house, you know? Kurt didn't buy a house. He was dealing with drug addiction when that was all raging. He was becoming a father. Then we didn't tour for a while, and then we got back together, and we did some tours, and Kurt was doing good. Kurt and Courtney were doing good because Courtney was pregnant, and she was showing, and that was a sweet time for them. We went, and we made up these shows because we cancelled this tour—we played Scandinavia, and that was nice. But, you know, then trying to deal with that fame . . .

COURTNEY: Well, people believe that I'm mostly upset [about the profile in the September 1992 issue of *Vanity Fair*] because it said I did heroin when I was pregnant, which was accurate. I did do heroin when I was pregnant, and then I stopped. When I found out I was pregnant, I got some Buprenorphine. I tapered off of

"[Kurt] was an exemplary father."—WENDY

heroin, and I didn't do heroin any more than anybody would from the moment they found out they were pregnant. And I didn't really struggle with it because it wasn't . . . you know, I stopped. I sweated bullets for a few nights. But there was an intervention in that period of time where a couple of people were trying to get me to get an abortion, and Kurt and me left in absolute disgust. We were furious. Bullshit, bullshit, bullshit, bullshit. I studied everything you can study online and offline about opiates in the early, like, first six weeks, and I knew [the baby] would be fine.

WENDY: I remember the article coming out. I remember the backlash [on] Courtney and Kurt. It was just . . . everything started going out of control.

COURTNEY: It emasculated [Kurt]. You know, because the piece made him vulnerable. And so the guilt I felt about making him look emasculated . . . if it had just been picking on me, it would've hurt. But it picked on him. And not only that—it had an effect. And the effect was my kid was born, and there's social workers all over the fucking hospital, carrying *Vanity Fair* around. Look, if it had been in *National Enquirer*, it wouldn't have been a big deal. In fact, it was in the *Globe*: "Rock Star's Baby Born a Junkie." You know, and that's about it. It was *Vanity Fair* and the *Globe.* But she wasn't born addicted to anything.

WENDY: [Kurt] was an exemplary father. He was wonderful with her.

TOP A still from a Stefan Nadelman animation sequence

OPPOSITE As the scandal around Courtney's heroin use grew, salacious stories filled newspapers and magazines around the world

Nirvana tot bounces back from dru...

SHOCK ro...
of Nirvan...
new baby...
his wife g...
binge durin...
Courtney L...

NIRVANA STAR KURT'S BABY BORN A DRUG ADDICT

NIRVANA star Kurt Cobain has become a dad—but his baby girl was born addicted to drugs.

The singer's tiny daughter Frances went cold turkey in hospital after his heroin addict girlfriend Courtney Love gave premature birth last week.

The heroin substitute methadone, which had been given to Courtney to ease her craving, poisoned the tot's bloodstream.

During her pregnancy Courtney confessed to a drug binge with Kurt, 25, who is headlining the Reading Rock Festival this weekend with Nirvana.

Hooked

Strange Love

Are Courtney Love, lead diva of the postpunk band Hole, and her husband, Nirvana heartthrob Kurt Cobain, the grunge John and Yoko? Or the next Sid and Nancy? LYNN HIRSCHBERG reports for Vanity Fair.

Daddy Kurt quits drugs

KURT Cobain—whose daughter Frances was born last month addicted to heroin—has quit drugs.

The Nirvana singer says: "Holding my baby is the best drug in the world."

Phone message from Kurt to Journalist Victoria Clarke:

This is Kurt Cobain. I have a lot of things to say to you. A lot of fucking things to say to you. You parasitic, little fucking cunts. You're not writing about my band. You're writing about how jealous you are of my wife. You have absolutely no fucking idea what you are doing. You will find out. I don't care that this is a recorded threat. I'm at the end of my rope. Never been more fucking serious in my life.

"We played with her all the time. Hung out with her all the time. She was always a part of his physical being."—COURTNEY

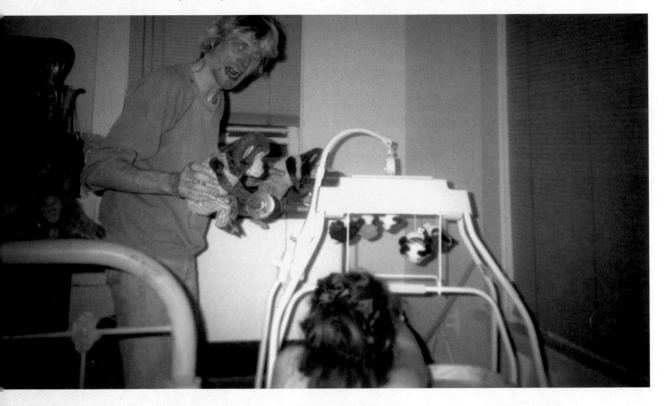

TOP, OPPOSITE, AND FOLLOWING PAGES Kurt adjusts to life as a father in these candid photos

COURTNEY: [Kurt was] great. Absolutely great. I mean, you know, look, there's functional junkies all over this town, right? In infancy you're dealing with a little bundle that just shits and laughs and cries. And so, you know, it's like we had good nannies who were very, very, very helpful. And we were very tactile with her. We played with her all the time. Hung out with her all the time. She was always a part of his physical being. He was super tactile with her. And, you know, it must've made a subconscious impression upon her although she doesn't have any conscious memory of him. On a Freudian level, there's got to be some memory impression, you know,

of him. So I think he'd have made a great father. And at the Rock and Roll Hall of Fame, I really asked myself for the first time, probably ever, honestly, "Would we still be married today?" I don't know if we would still be married. Because I don't know if we would've made it out of being two junkies. I know I would've made it out.

JENNY: I think a lot of people, Courtney included, thought that once this child came along, this little girl, that he would be a totally different person. But he went to kind of the dark side about it—"I'm not good enough" or whatever, even though that was kind of an excuse.

124

I chose to put myself in a position which requires the highest form of responsibility a person can have. A responsibility that should not be dictated by thinking what I should rather want to take on this responsibility. Every time I see a television show that has dying children or seeing a testimonial by a parent who recently lost their child I can't help but cry. The thought of losing my baby haunts me every day.

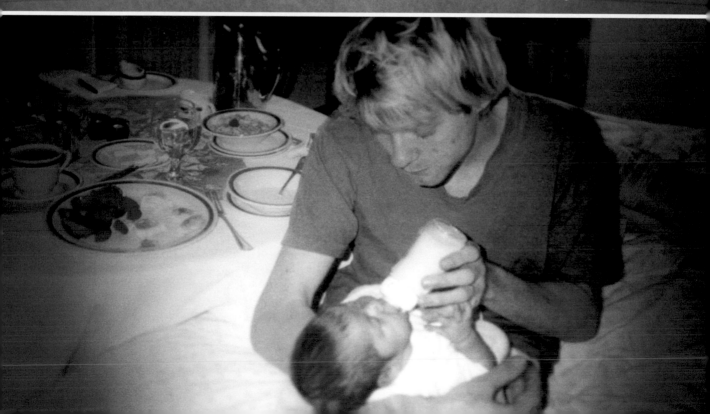

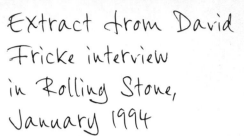

Extract from David Fricke interview in Rolling Stone, January 1994

KURT: No, my father and I are completely different people. I know that I'm capable of showing a lot more affection than my dad was. I mean, even if Courtney and I were to get a divorce, I would never allow us to be in a situation where there are bad vibes between us in front of her. If there's anything we're determined to do, it's to give Frances as much love as we can. I mean, if anything is going to stop me from pursuing this rock-and-roll thing, it's going to be her because I don't want her to be screwed up because of that. I don't know what's going to happen in the next few years . . . It's—it's kind of scary.

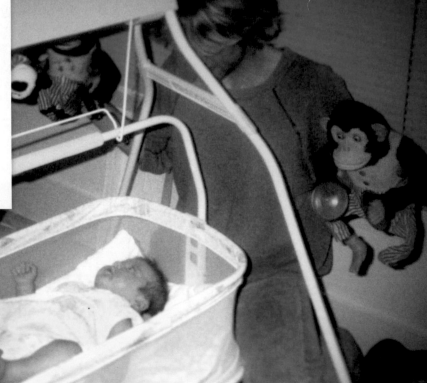

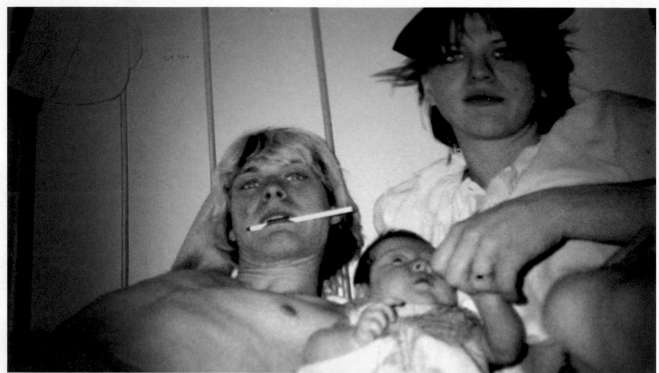

I sway back and forth between taking advantage of my position and giving up. Self appointed judges of review giving those with similar profit and potential the confidence to quit.

"He would puke for hours until there was blood coming up, and nobody knew what it was." —COURTNEY

COURTNEY: Just to backtrack a second, he had a terrible, terrible stomach condition that he did not inform me of before we were married. I'm not saying I wouldn't of married him, but there were three endoscopies I remember before Frances was even born. [He had to drink] this purple dye; they [stuck] a thing down there; no one could figure out what was wrong with him, and [his condition came], and it went without anything to do with stress. So it could be a great day or a shitty day, and it would come, and it would be horrible, and he would be in the bathroom on the floor throwing up. Did the heroin make it worse? That's the million-dollar question. I have no fucking idea. You know, when [Kurt] got off [heroin], all he would do is complain and complain and complain. But, listen, man, I'm telling you. He would puke for hours until there was blood coming up, and nobody knew what it was. He thought it was Lou Gehrig's disease, that it was

going to be a disease named after him. His mother claims she had it when she was a young woman. Frances had it one time at the hospital, and I went, "Oh, holy shit, holy shit, holy shit. Don't let this happen." And it never happened again.

WENDY: We never did figure out what it was. It started out as just vomiting. I just started vomiting. Everybody thought I had the flu. And then it wouldn't stop—I mean, like, every fifteen minutes I would throw up. I was seventeen. So, I had two episodes like that before Don and I got married. I got married at eighteen. And then I was in and out of the hospital until I was twenty-six. And I had to go because I would dehydrate.

KRIST: I think what was happening with him was physical. He was struggling with addiction, and that's tough. It takes its toll. And so then he would go on a binge, and then he'd have to clean up. He'd have

to go straight—he'd have to detox, kick, that whole thing. It was just hard for him. If he would have never done heroin, he'd still be alive today. But it was just [like the lyric from "Aneurysm"], "I love you so much it makes me sick / come on over and shoot the shit." "I love you so much it makes me sick / overdo it and have a fit." What a jerk, for writing that. I shouldn't call him a jerk, but those are nasty lyrics. But I guess he's not romanticizing it, right? He's talking about heroin, it's as plain as day. "I love you so much it makes me sick." There you have it. And it's too bad.

WENDY: Every week it got worse. And sometimes he would come home, I think, to hide. And it was really bad. He started getting sores, and he was losing weight and nodding out. And I was pretty sure he knew I knew, but I decided one time to just confront him. And so I went up to his bedroom, and he was sitting on the side of the bed. And he was just crying because I had just arrived, and he knew it was breaking my heart. But I talked to him about it and everything that I had learned about heroin. And I asked him if it, if he was at the stage if where he was addicted to the needle prick. And he burst into tears. He was just ashamed.

COURTNEY: Krist and him were pretty tight. Dave got more and more remote and wasn't around very much, so Kurt knew what he had in Dave, which was an amazing fucking drummer. Kurt wanted a fourth member, a happy person. He wanted somebody to connect the band, somebody to make the band feel more like a band, and we thought of everyone. I thought of my friend Pat Smear, and Pat was working at the SST Superstore

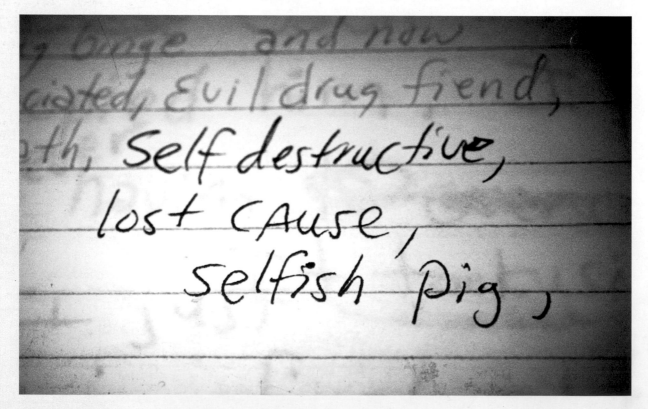

134

"I think he made music that was so sensitive and angry, [but] the reality of his life, you know, was shame."—WENDY

[a punk rock music store]. And Pat could handle the vicissitudes of somebody being on heroin. That's really Pat's service to Nirvana—that he didn't care if Kurt was on heroin. He just didn't give a shit, whereas there was all this judgment and casting of aspersions and complaining to the manager about Kurt's roiling heroin problem, which, by the way, hadn't even reared its head yet. Wait till you get to the end of his life. Then it's bad, you know what I mean? And I've said this before and I'll say it again on record, that when Kurt did heroin, he went all the way to the wall.

WENDY: [He'd be] crying, "I want to quit the band. I can't stand the guys. I can't stand any more of this." And then [he told me that] at the end of a show in France this young boy came up [to him]—[Kurt] was crying when he told me this—[he said] "Mom, he couldn't have been more than twelve, and he came out of the audience with a piece of foil and opened it up with a grin on his face, saying, 'Look, Kurt, look what I got.'" Either to give it to him or show him that he was doing it. And he said, "If I'm causing this, you know, I've got to stop." I think he made music that was so sensitive and angry, [but] the reality of his life, you know, was shame. Really, a lot of shame. Because he knew that he was influencing and affecting. He didn't realize he had that kind of clout with such young children.

COURTNEY: He didn't want to destroy his career. There's this huge mythology about *In Utero* and how the record company hated the mixes. That's just

TOP As seen in Kurt Cobain: Montage of Heck, *a journal sketch by Kurt makes reference to his drug habit and Courtney's apparent sobriety*

bullshit. He made that up. He liked the story. He loved good myths about himself. And he was sensitive, truly, and so he would make a good mythology about it: He wasn't ambitious. He never asked for this. Corporate magazines still suck. Whatever. You know what I mean? Like, fuck off. But then the problem was his execution wasn't all that great. So in terms of interviews, like, live television interviews, he knows what the answer should be, but he doesn't quite get it across because he's not being truly honest, and the best way to do an interview is to just tell the fucking truth. If you're going to lie, believe your lie. It's like me sitting there in customs with heroin on me, and it's, like, I believed I didn't have any heroin on me and that's how I'm not in jail to this day, you know?

KIM: The Kurt that he was giving to the media was, you know, "Let's see if I can fool them. Let's see if I can tell a story."

I think in the earlier days he would tell total bullshit lies and make up stuff. But that's just because those weren't people that he was close to. With other people, he was a little more outgoing. He was silly, he was funny, he was kind of a practical joker. And what people saw in public was like, "Oh, I guess I have to be kind of depressed." I think that's why he didn't want to do interviews anymore.

JENNY: One thing that he said to me that was so ironic was that I asked him about some songs that he was writing, and I said, "Do you know where you came up with this?" And he said, "You gotta throw in these words and make it all rhyme." So many people think that a lot of the things were from his heart, but in a way, a lot of them were just made up things, you know what I mean? Like the "under the bridge" song ["Something in the Way"], I can't remember what it's called. It made people feel sorry for

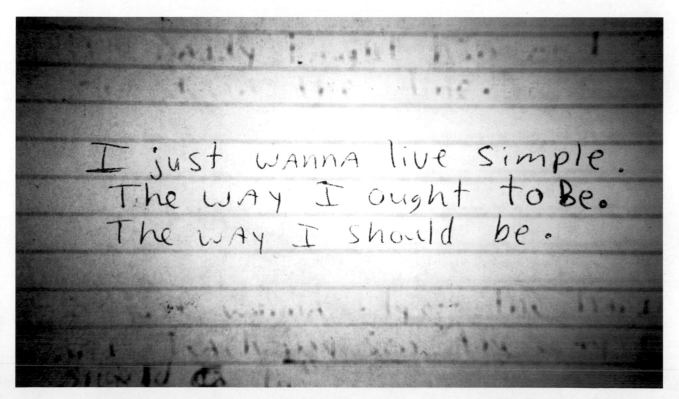

I just wanna live simple.
The way I ought to be.
The way I should be.

him, and I think people wanted to feel sorry for him. And I think he liked that. Because he was so sensitive.

KIM: That's the bridge that we would go and get stoned under. Do graffiti, hang out, you know . . . No one ever lived under that bridge. He had times where he ran away from home and went and lived at a friend's house for a couple of weeks. But I don't think he was, like, completely displaced. He always could come home.

"I called him the windmill, because he would say something and a few minutes later he'd contradict it."—KRIST

COURTNEY: He'd also refer to heroin in the past tense: "I used to be a junkie, I used to be a junkie," when he was high as a kite. Because he was aware of being a role model to kids, and he didn't want kids on heroin. That was something we expressed together—just deny that you're high even if you're nodding into your soup. Deny that you're high. Deny, deny, deny. What can they say?

KRIST: I called him the windmill, because he would say something and a few minutes later he'd contradict it. I'd say to him, "Do you know what you just said?" And he'd just look at me and laugh, like, *Ahahaha.* Like he knew.

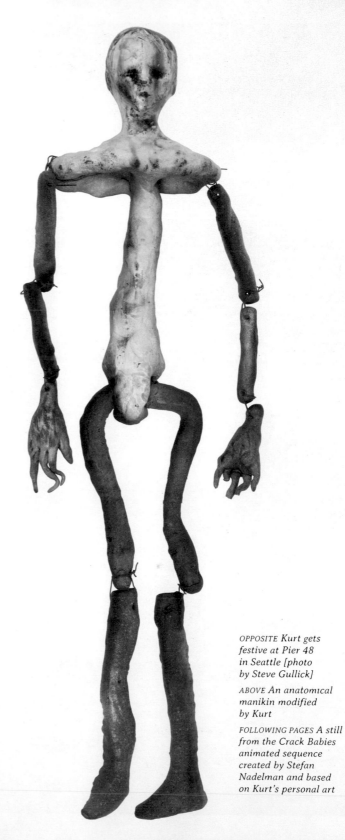

OPPOSITE Kurt gets festive at Pier 48 in Seattle [photo by Steve Gullick]

ABOVE An anatomical manikin modified by Kurt

FOLLOWING PAGES A still from the Crack Babies animated sequence created by Stefan Nadelman and based on Kurt's personal art

AIN'T IT A SHAME

COURTNEY: The happiest I ever saw him in terms of fitting in with the rock star thing—close to his death, bodyguard, limousine, hanging out with the other bands, a few lines being chopped, models—[was at the Hollywood Rock festival in Rio]. He had such a good time in Rio. He had such a good time because he was being a rock star. I tried to talk him into having a threesome. He wouldn't do it. He was too much of a monogamist. That was his argument. I was, like, "Let's have a threesome. She's a model. Just say that you had it. Like, you're a rock star. I mean, I'm not even gay. Let's do it; she's hot." Wouldn't do it.

KIM: Kurt and I are both extremely monogamous and, you know, he would be just completely distraught over any kind of infidelity if he was with someone that was supposed to be his lifetime partner. Because he couldn't fathom ever cheating on someone that he was in love with. He was a monogamous person, and he wanted the same from his partner. Whoever he was in love with, whoever he married, if someone was not faithful to him, it would completely destroy him.

COURTNEY: I almost [cheated] one time and he knew it, and I don't know how he knew it. The plan didn't ever go anywhere, so it was just—nothing happened, but I was

104th Year No. 219   Grays Harbor   Co

Nirvana star Kurt Cobain out of coma

By The Daily World staff & The Associated Press

ROME — Kurt Cobain, lead singer for Nirvana, the chart-topping rock group that was born in Aberdeen, emerged

ANSA, an Italian news age cy, said Cobain, 27, became after combining a large dose Roipnol with champagne.

Roipnol is used mostly f insomnia cases and is not ca ried by many Italian pharm

tired, and I wasn't as monogamous as he is. I'm a big flirt; I'll flirt with a chair. I never, never cheated on him, but I certainly thought about it one time in London. And I could've done it, and the response to it was he took sixty-seven Rohypnols and ended up in a coma because I thought about cheating on him. I mean, fuck. You're kidding? Like, that's how psychic he was? I didn't want to have sex that night because I had taken some of the Rohypnols, [so]

OPPOSITE Kurt onstage in New York during the In Utero tour [photo by Kevin Mazur/ WireImage/Getty Images]

TOP A clipping from Aberdeen, WA, newspaper, The Daily World, reports Kurt's overdose in Rome

I went to bed. I just wanted to sleep and not have sex. And I woke up, and he was in his coat, and he had, like, a six-page suicide note that wasn't all that nice. It wasn't horrible, but it wasn't all that nice. It was like, "You've rejected me," *da da da da*. I can't remember. I gave it to the Seattle Police Department. I don't know why. It had nothing to do with his actual death.

WENDY: And where could Kurt go? What rehab center could he go to where the paparazzi or the magazines weren't going to find him? The newspapers? There was nowhere. He couldn't have that addiction [be] private. And it's his own fault. I couldn't watch the last thing that he did in '93. It was in Seattle, a concert that was done in Seattle, because he was so messed up. I couldn't believe they let him go on in that state. It was the most horrifying thing I've ever seen, where he was so out of it, and he was

allowed to continue, and that just broke my heart. I had to turn it off. I couldn't watch it. And then four months later he was dead. And that's the music industry for you. You know, they knew that when he put a foot on that stage that he was completely messed up. I mean it was the worst I've ever seen him.

COURTNEY: After Rome, [where Kurt took the overdose], he was just like the walking dead. He just wasn't himself. It had just gotten to the point where he couldn't function. I called for help. I needed help. I didn't know what to do. I tried to grab his legs because he was going to meet some dealer, and he just kept walking and dragged me across the gravel because he wanted to get in the car so bad. And then he could barely drive the fucking thing, and he dropped Frances. And when he dropped Frances—she didn't fall on her head or anything, but he dropped her—and I was, like, "This is the fucking

OPPOSITE A still from animation by Stefan Nadelman, based on Kurt's art. The original composition is known to fans as the cover for Nirvana's Incesticide *album*

BELOW Stefan Nadelman's animated rendition of collage art from Kurt's archive

"After Rome he was just like the walking dead."—COURTNEY

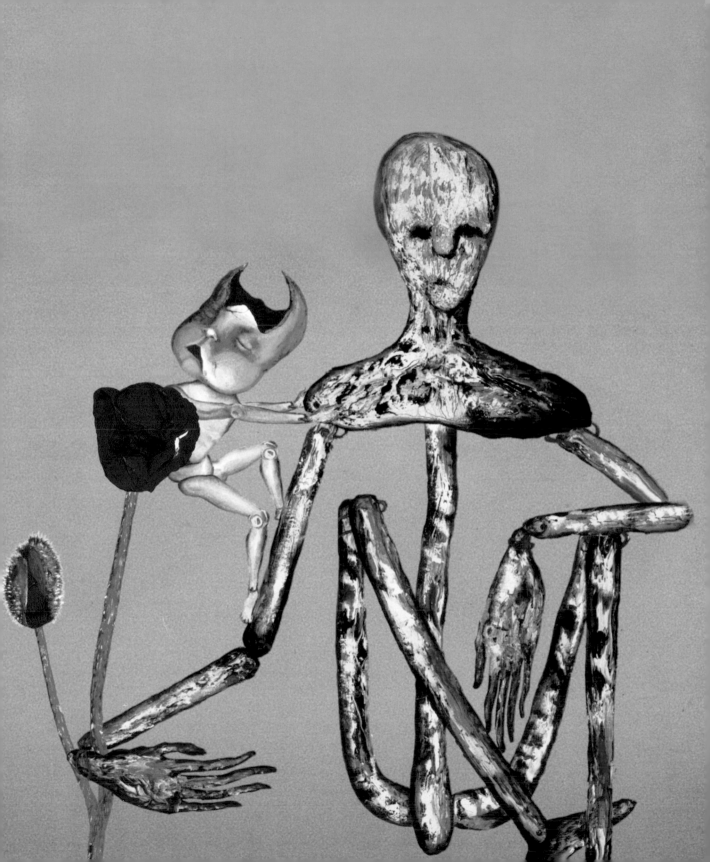

end, man. You gotta fucking stop. You gotta fucking stop, or this is the end. You can't drop the baby, no." He wasn't, like, my best friend anymore. He was somewhere else. You know, his head was somewhere else. Where drugs mattered more than anything.

KIM: Mom says that I was there for something. For the, you know, pseudo-intervention thing.

COURTNEY: I forget [everybody] who was there. It just went bad, and I went up to the greenhouse where he was hiding and hugged him, and I was, like, "You know you don't have to go anywhere if you don't want to." And then plane tickets were purchased, and he really wanted to. "I really wanna stop," he said. "I really wanna stop. I wanna stop doing drugs. I really wanna stop." And, you know, I mean, it was your average shitty intervention, like on TV. I mean, it wasn't like people sat around with lists. It wasn't like that. It was, like, this

is a fucking emergency, this needs triage, you are bleeding. You need to go to rehab. We had had interventions before, [like] the intervention to stop me having a baby. I think maybe he thought I had turned on him, but I hadn't. So, I'm not a fan of interventions at all. I mean, obviously. I would never do that again. I would do it differently, but I don't know what I would do other than have a full-time sober guy that was about six-foot-nine, who was too big for Kurt to dump, who would go along with [him] when he went to get his drugs and make sure he didn't overdose. You know, I mean, it was like we couldn't turn back time. From that time in Rome onward, we couldn't go back. We could always rewind before, you know, we could always buck up, rally, everything's okay. But from that moment . . .

WENDY: It wasn't something that I ever worried about before, say, 1992. After that I was, like, really worried about him. About suicide.

OPPOSITE Stills from an animated sequence created by Stefan Nadelman, based on Kurt's personal art

TOP Rough sketches from Kurt's journals

KRIST: It was a different world after 1991, 1992. There were Democrats back in the White House. We had this young president. It was a good time to be idealistic about things. But by 1994 it was all over. There was a Gingrich revolution. Kurt was dead.

COURTNEY: Once he said, "How old am I?" And it might've been after Rome, but I think it was before. And I said, "You're twenty-seven." And he goes, "Oh." And I went, "Oh, shut up," because we'd talked about [Jim] Morrison and [Jimi] Hendrix and [Janis] Joplin and [the age] twenty-seven [at which they died]. And I got a kind of creepy feeling. And then there's the guns, and the guns are a fucking nightmare, but he said it was for protection. We did get threats, and he felt like he was going to get shot. You know, I mean, he was really paranoid about that.

KRIST: When he killed himself, he was out of his mind. The last time I saw him he was out of his mind on heroin, and there were people at that house that were the same way. They were just really into heroin. And they all survived, and he didn't. He killed himself is what he did. He just couldn't deal with it anymore.

COURTNEY: A lot of people are really too quick to call him bipolar or depressive. Obviously depressive but bipolar or manic? He wasn't manic depressive. I would've known.

KIM: That fine line between genius and madness? I think he was right on the border there. I mean, he more than likely had some type of, you know, depression of some sort, just from feeling alienated. I don't know if he had any kind of, like, actual mental illness. I don't think so.

JENNY: I think he was really afraid that Frances was gonna hear all kinds of negative things about him, and he was so sensitive to her. In his mind, I feel like

OPPOSITE AND TOP Simple but expressive artwork by Kurt gives insight into the many facets of his personality

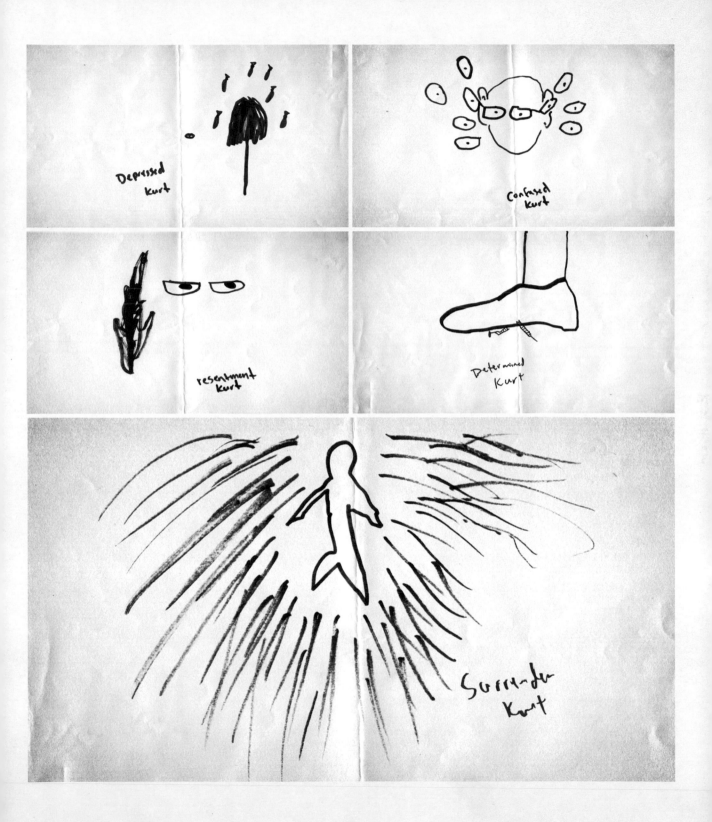

he thought she was better off without him. Which, I know, [is] very hard to understand. He just couldn't handle it, even though that's what he wanted more than anything. Those insecurities and all that was still with him, and he was never good enough in his own mind. And I don't know what made him that way. He was the first-born grandchild of this huge family. He was adorable.

KRIST: I was shocked. Then I thought about it, like, "Kurt's such a quitter." He left his daughter. What a quitter, you know what I mean? I was angry at him with that suicide. For a lot of things. That he just quit like that. He could've done anything he wanted to do. But you know, his judgment, being so high . . . It was bad judgment. I don't know why he did it. Maybe he was humiliated.

COURTNEY: Why couldn't I or Kurt get clean for the baby? Yeah, I don't know. Maybe we were failures as parents. I don't know. I mean, we kept trying.

KIM: He thought everybody would be better off without him. He thought that, you know, Courtney would get clean, and Frances would have this great mother if he wasn't in the picture because he thought that he was the problem. And it was more the drugs that were the problem. They controlled everything.

COURTNEY: I think feeling that it would be better for Frances is where he went really wrong. He was very, very much in love with his daughter, and I think that he truly thought she'd be better off without him. And he truly felt abandoned, and that predates me. And he truly felt that the world would be a better place without him, and he truly had the balls to do it. But [Frances] thinks she's related to [the equivalent of] Santa Claus, so you know,

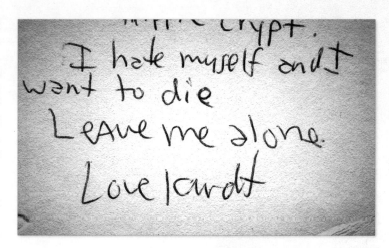

it didn't have the desired effect. But it never does.

KRIST: But it's all 20/20 hindsight. With the skills I had, I think I did the best I could do. I hope so. But, you know, reading the lyrics, in hindsight you're, like, "Wow." But again, it was such a whirlwind that we were caught up in. And going into the whole thing with limited skills, I just have a world of regrets. I think about it all the time. It's not far from my mind, and it's painful. And, you know, I live a comfortable life. I'm blessed with that because of my association with Kurt and Nirvana. So I'm not complaining, but I'm also not in denial either about the reality of what happened. It's a lot of painful memories that I can never forget.

DON: It's just such a waste. Because it seemed to me like he had the world by the balls, and then he does what he did, just give it up. I don't understand. Wish I could've. In hindsight, you wish you would've realized or could've done something to make things different for him. I think we tried. Chad and I even went over there a couple times to try to get with him and stuff like that. You know, nothing happens. You just don't understand, I guess.

TOP A scrawled note from Kurt begins with the phrase that almost became the title of In Utero

OPPOSITE AND FOLLOWING PAGES Stills from an animated sequence created by Stefan Nadelman, based on Kurt's personal art

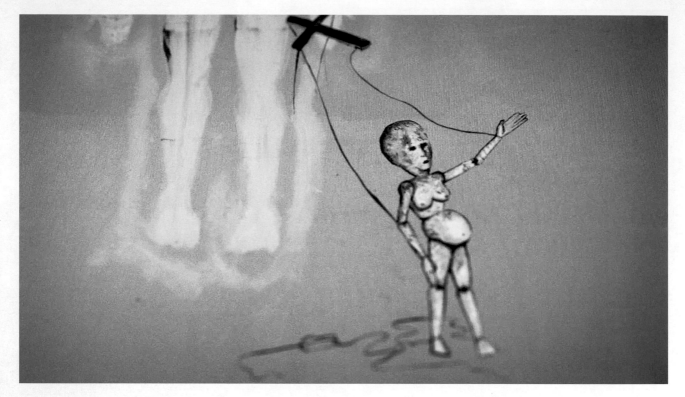

JENNY: It hurts all of us, the many bad things Kurt said about Don. It hurts the whole family, and I wish there were some way, you know, that could stop. But in any tragedy like that—that horrible blaming—if you're a decent person, you're gonna blame yourself. Because you want to have fixed it, and nobody could fix him. You know there was no fixing. And sending him off to rehab all the time didn't fix him, and he didn't want to stop. And I really think he got to the point where he knew that he couldn't. So I think one day he just decided to give up. Does that sound weird?

COURTNEY: Like I said, he was happy in Rio, because he was treated like a proper rock star with all the trappings. Those trappings can be really fun, and I think if he had embraced the trappings from the beginning, he'd had had a more fun ride, man. You know, our little generation wasn't allowed to be successful, and if

we were, we were supposed to do it on the sly. I mean, now it's, like, Dave lives in a mansion, you know? I mean, Krist still herds goats or something, but we weren't allowed to sort of live in mansions and have bodyguards when we needed bodyguards. And then Seattle was just gloomy because there was nobody there to talk to. But, you know, I was really happy playing house with Kurt, like, that's what I wanted to do. I like shopping for weird shit, but otherwise I just liked hanging out with Kurt.

KRIST: Kurt made an enduring body of work and it's going to last a long, long time and he's already an artist in the upper echelon of creative people who changed the world, maybe not society, but like one person at a time for whatever they want to find in [the music]. Good art invites you into its world. [You're] invited into the world that he made, that weird world that Kurt Cobain [created

I Kurt Donald Cobain, being of sound mind hereby state my last will and testimony.

Custody of my daughter frances B Cobain goes to Courtney Cobain (my wife) and in the event of her death, frances' custody goes to Danny Goldberg and Rosemary Carroll of los Angeles CA. If they decline, frances' custody will go to my sister Kimberly Cobain of Seattle WA. It is against our will to have france's custody to be turned over to Kurts father Don Cobain or Courtneys mother

with] writhing bodies [and] tragic broken characters, but somehow it's beautiful and compelling.

WENDY: You know, the public had him for three-and-a-half years; I had him for twenty-seven. And there is so much more to his life. I mean, three-and-a-half years out of twenty-seven years. He was a wonderful human being. Caring and loving. And, what happened to him, he got seduced. He got sucked into hell. And then that's what happens when you let that barrier down one too many times. Like, "Ah, what the hey, I'll do it." And that's what happened.

KIM: That was, what, three years? Maybe four of his years that he was doing drugs, becoming famous and dealing with the public and all that? That was such a small part of him. But it was huge to everyone else. It's giant to everyone else because that's when everyone all of a sudden knew who he was. Or thought they, you know, knew.

KRIST: I miss that guy. I think about him all the time.

COURTNEY: The last line in that suicide note is something like, "It'll be better without me." And it's just been carnage. It's been twenty years of just carnage. You know, it's just a nightmare.

KRIST: He was the coolest, the nicest—he was right on. He was a good person. He was really good. And he could be a good friend. And it's just too bad what happened. God, I just hate it when I think about it. It just makes me sick. It's just fucked up. You know what I mean? He was a good person. And Kurt's legacy is in connecting with individuals who were born after he died. He's still connecting with people. It's in his vision, which is so powerful and so compelling to so many people. It's that somebody says, "That music changed my life." Somehow there was a person who was going through something, and the music spoke to them, and they saw the world in a new way.

OPPOSITE Kurt at the Four Seasons hotel in Seattle [photo by Charles Peterson]

TOP An extract from Kurt's will

FOLLOWING PAGES AND CREDITS PAGE Stills from Hisko Hulsing animated sequences

CREDITS
Original artwork Hisko Hulsing
Graphic treatments by Stefan Nadelman,
based on artwork by Kurt Cobain
Production liaison James Smith
Production assistant Claire Gavin

ACKNOWLEDGMENTS
The filmmakers would like to thank Debra Eisenstadt, Skylar Morgen, Max
Morgen, Jasper Morgen, Wendy O'Connor, Kim Cobain, Don Cobain, Jenny
Cobain, Krist Novoselic, Courtney Love, Dave Grohl, Frances Bean Cobain,
David Byrnes, Michael Meisel, Aurelie De Troyer & the Universal team,
Sheila Nevins, Sara Bernstein and the HBO team, Jackie Eckhouse, Jessica
Berman-Bogdan, Sarah Copas, and Ryan Loeffler.

Insight Editions would like to thank End of Music LLC, Frances Bean Cobain,
and Courtney Love.

INSIGHT
EDITIONS
PO Box 3088
San Rafael, CA 94912
www.insighteditions.com

Find us on Facebook: www.facebook.com/InsightEditions
Follow us on Twitter: @insighteditions

PUBLISHER: Raoul Goff
ACQUISITIONS: Steve Jones
EXECUTIVE EDITOR: Vanessa Lopez
ART DIRECTOR: Chrissy Kwasnik
DESIGNER: Jon Glick
SENIOR EDITOR: Chris Prince
PRODUCTION EDITOR: Rachel Anderson
PRODUCTION MANAGER: Jane Chinn
EDITORIAL ASSISTANT: Greg Solano

ROOTS of PEACE   REPLANTED PAPER
Insight Editions, in association with Roots of Peace, will plant two trees
for each tree used in the manufacturing of this book. Roots of Peace is
an internationally renowned humanitarian organization dedicated to
eradicating land mines worldwide and converting war-torn lands into
productive farms and wildlife habitats. Roots of Peace will plant two million
fruit and nut trees in Afghanistan and provide farmers there with the skills
and support necessary for sustainable land use.

Manufactured in U.S.A. by Insight Editions

10 9 8 7 6 5 4 3 2 1